James Keating, Ph.D.

Pure
Heart
Clear Conscience

Living a Catholic
Moral Life

Our Sunday Visitor Publishing Division
Our Sunday Visitor, Inc.
Huntington, Indiana 46750

ISBN: 0-87973-572-4
LCCCN: 98-67815

Cover design by Monica Watts

PRINTED IN THE UNITED STATES OF AMERICA
572

Dedication

To Mom, Dad, Collean, Kevin, Eileen, Maureen, Peggy, Marianne, and of course Liam Solanus.

Acknowledgments
Thanks to Elizabeth Kampmeier, M.Div., Theology
Faculty Research Assistant at the Pontifical College
Josephinum, for all the work she did to help prepare the text;
and to Dennis Bliss, Ph.D., for his careful reading of the text.

Contents

Preface

Being good is our heart's desire. We only know happiness when we center our lives within a relationship to what is good. Becoming a good person is about recognizing what is morally true and then identifying those moral truths again and again and loving them. To recognize what is good is to see that we are not the center of reality. Our Creator is the center of all reality, and our heart's desire to be good is simply our desire to be faithful to our relationship with God. Our dignity as persons hinges upon that relationship and our desire to live it out faithfully.

The Christian moral life is not only about choosing. It is also about *being chosen*. Fundamentally it is about receiving the grace and love of God and responding to that divine love. One of the oldest and most beautiful of moral truths is that we are changed by what we love. Our characters are molded according to what we have paid attention to. The often-heard sentiment regarding one's action, "Oh, it was nothing," cannot be true in the moral realm. Every considered behavior affects the character of the one performing the act, for good or ill. This does not mean that every act carries the same weight of importance, but simply acknowledges that our actions count. We are creating our characters through free choice. We do not create what is good or evil. Goodness and evil create us. We do not create what is good simply by our personal choosing;

being good revolves around being a faithful creature of God. We do not create moral goodness; we are created to embrace it.

When we approach the moral life from the perspective of someone whom God has chosen to love, we see that moral living is very personal and not something imposed upon us by the Church. The urgent need today for those who wish to properly understand Christian moral living is to [re-]establish contact with God in Christ through the power of the Holy Spirit. The parish community facilitates this contact with God. There is nothing isolated about moral conversion or formation. We have received our Christian identity through the Church and we embrace that ecclesial identity in order to know freedom. The ruin of moral living is to reduce it to a private activity, or to enlarge it to an overarching corporatism that refuses to respect the individual or serve the individual's good. Ultimately, the authentic moral life is lived in the tension of being a person in community and being a community of persons.

Intentional moral formation cannot, however, be the product of a general community (such as "I am an American" or "I am middle-class"). It has to be more specific and enfolded within relationships, symbols, and rituals that celebrate, define, and enable persons to grow beyond egoism into relatedness with God and others. For most of us, this moral formation happens best in the family and in the parish, the two communities that encompass the primary means for encountering the holy within the ordinary existence of daily living. God may gift us with extraordinary experiences of His love during a walk in the woods, or while driving our car, or as we collaborate with a co-worker on a project. But these are exactly as I have identified them — extraordinary. To remain aware of human dignity, our unique worth as persons, we are to remain before God in the midst of our family and in the midst of the parish as the body of Christ. These communities are the ordinary locales for moral and spiritual growth; it is here that God touches us with the truth about Him and ourselves. For so many people it is their spouse who gives the best spiritual direction, or it is their child or brother or sister who pricks the conscience. For so many people it is the encounter with the Word of God preached from the pulpit or the reception of Christ in the Eucharist that awakens them to goodness. The first step to moral conversion is to remember the dignity of our own and others' identity before God. We are called to respect this dignity within the ordinary circumstances of home, parish, and professional life. If we miss these calls within the ordinariness of daily existence, we miss the divine invitation to holiness.

In this book I want to share a vision of moral living which calls persons back into their religious identity, so that they can hear the call of conscience from within an explicit relationship with God. For those called to Catholicism, moral development occurs most effectively when one is faithful to that call. To ignore our religious identity is to ignore the only reality that lasts into eternity: the love of God within the midst of community. Being good *is* our heart's desire, as persons called into relationship with God. Moral formation is about recognizing that we are chosen by God in love, knowing we have to respond to that divine love, and then being formed by that relationship of love.

1

Is It Boring Being Good?

There is nothing more interesting for a person than living a moral life. This sounds somewhat absurd because all around us people espouse the myth that being immoral is really exciting. Certainly immoral behavior gives us pleasure, or power, or even prestige (think of how [in]famous people become when they engage in immoral behavior and publicize it: "No publicity is bad publicity," the saying goes). But in the long run immoral behavior is boring.[1] This is just the opposite of what we thought was true in high school. In our distorted thinking, the good kids were the "nerds." They studied, listened to their parents, went to bed on time, and attended church. The bad kids "ate, drank, and were merry." They stayed up all night and experimented with drugs or alcohol. Maybe they stole things from local stores or engaged in premarital sex. That was considered the good life! How do we feel about those activities now, as adults?

As adults we may certainly be tempted to greed, lust, or gluttony, especially when the predictable routine of daily living begins to define our lives. But do we seriously think these temptations are the answers to achieving a life of enduring meaning? Our hearts tell us otherwise. Over time our hearts tell us that immoral actions are wrong even as they continue to hold us fascinated. It is this fascination that deludes us into thinking that immoral behavior is capable of quelling the restlessness in our hearts. But the fascination is simply a facade, a shining silver wrapper attracting one to an object with no depth or content — moral evil. Despite appearances, only the authentic moral life can pacify the restless heart.

Being good is a more interesting life because in it we focus our affections upon that which is worthy of our love: the true, the good, and the beautiful. We need to love persons, experiences, and things that are dignified because in our loving them we become like them.[2] Immoral behavior is ultimately boring simply because the nature of evil is about isolation, self-absorption, and emptiness. This emptiness is the opposite of what we know human life to be truly about — relatedness. Evil's power is most penetrating in those times when we are confused about what it means to be human, when we forget that we are the beloved of God. In our confusion, evil tempts us, calls us, and undermines our sense of self-knowledge by whispering words of insecurity, fear, and hate. Evil has a power, and its power is real. It is bigger than we are and can "lap over us like waves pounding the seashore."[3]

To introduce the idea of moral evil, understood as that which pulls us away from God, I want to give three examples that will highlight its power and ultimately its emptiness: The evils of gossip and pornography are good examples of the emptiness of evil; selfishness is a good example of the loneliness evil fosters. If we understand our human identity as beloved of God and appropriate that love, we can better overcome the temptations to evil as presented by vices such as gossip, lust, and selfishness.

Gossip

The experience of being intrigued by gossip provides a good example of the power of evil's undertow. The invitation to gossip is itself fascinating, its whispered "let me tell you something" draws us in. Immediately we are readied to learn; we lean forward with eyes wide and emotions set on edge as we anticipate the news about another's demise, weakness, or humiliation. What are we being pulled into here? Why do we so easily yield to its power? We lunge into a gossip session because we know at the end of it we will have, if only for a moment, a clear sense of what we crave the most — an identity. We yield easily to gossip when we are filled with self-hate and insecurity. If I am gossiping about a person's illicit sex life, for example, or drug abuse, or both, I am assured at the end of gossiping that I can say, "Well, I may be many things, but at least I know I am not an adulterous drunk." This knowledge assuages our anxiety for a time, like having "just one" cigarette dulls the aching need of a person who is trying to quit smoking. Soon, however, this gossip fix will wear thin and the gossiper will again have to build a sense of self upon the ashes of another's reputation.

Gossip is not simply talking about others in their absence. It is talking about others and intending to revel in harmful and oftentimes unsubstantiated information regarding their character or behavior. It has a slanderous bent to it. When the gossip is over, the gossipers leave ashes behind. That is what inhabits evil: emptiness. Moral evil is boring because there is nothing in it. It is the black hole of the soul, sucking in all things negative, promising satisfaction, but leading us nowhere. This cycle winds down only if a person can become centered in one identity. Like the gossiper said, "I may be *many* things. . . ." A moral character born out of loving what is in accord with our Christian identity blunts the dispersing of our identity into many superficial factions. Our identity needs to be saved from the complete dissolution that can occur when we compare self to others in gossip. In the secure knowledge of who we are in Christ, there is little need for us to find our identity by impugning another's reputation.

Pornography

When I was a boy growing up near New York City, there was a tradition in some schools that when a boy turned eighteen he would get on the subway and head for Times Square to see a pornographic movie. It was a confused rite of passage celebrating the attainment of manhood. My high school days were before Walt Disney moved into Times Square to create the family entertainment zone that it is trying to be now. In pre-Disney days, men would stand outside the XXX theaters and entice boys into the movie, promising that the prettiest girls were found in "this and only this" theater. The circus of the Times Square and Forty-second Street theater barkers is a metaphor for a hallmark of evil — it promises more than it can ever deliver. The barkers enticed the boys into theaters with lies about the so-called happiness they claimed was to be found within. But once inside, the boys encountered a place reflective of its purpose: The theater was squalid, the clientele pathetic, and the feature film's quality resembled a bad home video. Since all pornographic sex is devoid of any substantive narrative, it wasn't long before many of the newly initiated young men felt bored by it all and left the theater before the movie ended. They became men, yes, but not because of this confused rite of passage (watching a pornographic movie) — they became men because they chose to leave the theater and reject its false promises.

If we use pornography and gossip as metaphors for moral evil, we see clearly that the power of evil lies in its capacity to promise more than it can ever deliver. It is an empty promise. Evil simply spins a web of new lies to capture those unsure of their own dignity and identity, those without a secure object of love. To struggle against moral evil, we need a firm sense of identity that is rooted in reality, the reality of God's love for us.

Selfishness

Another example of evil manifesting its character is the experience of selfishness. Selfishness is a disposition that promotes the ego's needs to the exclusion of others' needs. It is generated by fear and cannot risk empathy for others. Selfishness exhibits itself publicly through actions of taking, grabbing, and controlling the lives of others. Deep down, selfish people feel that no one loves them, even that they are undeserving of love; therefore, they must think double-time about themselves. The deluded thought is, "Unless I take what I need, I will have to go without." Here we come to the pathetic misperception of the selfish individual — that people are essentially alone. This belief becomes a self-fulfilling prophecy — selfish people end up alone. Only those who abandon self-absorption and adopt a self-giving life will be able to receive what they need. In other words, those who love and are loved are not forgotten because they make a space to receive gifts from others. Those who love are not self-sufficient; they leave spaces for others to approach, to offer gifts, to engage them. Hence, they are not alone. The selfish person, on the other hand, cannot risk leaving spaces, but must always take control and be in power due to the overwhelming fear of not being recognized by others. Selfishness begets loneliness.

Moreover, in our contemporary culture, selfishness is a sign of an identity defined by the possessions we lack rather than by our relationships. Not only does the selfish person take control of situations out of his or her fear of being forgotten, but also this habit of greediness can be exacerbated by the influence of media images of success and wealth. One can begin to think, "I just need *this* car, *this* kind of house in *this* location, *this* kind of body, hair, face," in order to be successful and happy. Advertising has bid us for so long to focus on what we lack, that we have actually come to identify ourselves by that which we do not possess but desire; hence, we have embraced our identity as consumers. We will go to great lengths to take and acquire things and experiences in order to feel good about who we are, when in reality so many (rich and middle-class) Americans do not lack for any material possessions. But advertisers spend billions of dollars to convince us that we need just one more thing. Print and television advertising is effective in forming our values and influencing behavior — why else would billions be spent if the TV image had no power to persuade, to change our behavior, and to influence what we think we lack and therefore need?

Simplifying one's life by choosing to own less is, first of all, an act of love for oneself. Simple living clears away the distractions that possessions can become and frees us to concentrate on relationships. Out of that freedom we will share our goods with the poor. This simple living, which puts relationships ahead of things, will not solve the problem of global poverty, but it will assist others in small ways and contribute to the development of the virtue of charity within us.

Recently, I experienced the pain of selfishness in my own relationship with my family. I had gone to the doctor for a routine physical and learned that I had a high cholesterol count. After inquiring about my diet, the doctor told me to cut out the high-fat and high-sugar foods and begin to snack on pretzels and diet soda. Even these were to be had in moderate amounts. Needless to say I was filled with anxiety. How could I go on without my regular intake of candy bars? One day at work after a month of dieting, I realized that I had done a good job of refraining from candy and decided that I deserved to celebrate. It crossed my mind that my wife, Marianne, could have at least remembered my heroic efforts at foregoing candy and cookies and recognized the anniversary in some way. This lack of recognition by my family made me feel *even more* deserving of a celebratory candy bar.

Is It Boring Being Good?

After teaching class I got in my car and drove toward home. On the way there I decided to stop and buy candy. I began to realize, however, that my giving in to these cravings was infantile, so I quickly decided to drive straight home. I then noticed that my gas gauge read empty. I *had* to stop and buy gas. Of course, I knew what awaited me within the convenience store at the gas station: candy. I pumped the gas and went in to pay the bill. I looked at the candy lining the counter near the cash register and quickly turned and left the store. I just as quickly returned and said to the attendant, "I'll have one of those candy bars, please." I again left the store and drove the car from its position in front of the gas pumps to a place behind the store. I parked and tore into the candy bar, devouring every bite. I threw the wrapper in the trash near the store, not wanting anyone to find the evidence. I returned to the car and began to drive home.

Suddenly, I felt anger rise within me. "If Marianne had remembered my dieting anniversary, I wouldn't have stooped so low as to buy the stupid candy bar." I was precariously close to thinking, "It's all her fault!" I pulled into the driveway, got out of the car, and noticed that the house was dark. As I entered the front door I glimpsed a faint light coming from the dining room, so I walked toward it. In the dining room I saw a small candle on the table; seated were my sons, Kristoffer and Jonathan, along with Marianne. "Congratulations!" they screamed. "You did it," said Kristoffer. Leaning on the candle was a greeting card and, next to the card, a candy bar. Needless to say it was the worst candy bar I had ever eaten. Guilt tastes very bitter.

The problem with selfishness is that it greedily *takes* what was meant to be *given*. How could I celebrate and be grateful during my family's recognition of my achievement when I had already grabbed what I thought no one was willing to give? The suffering of the selfish is the knowledge that their deepest desire — to be remembered in love — was about to be satisfied but, instead, became thwarted by their own hand. In the moral life we have to be willing to receive from the heart of God the gifts, graces, and assistance needed to become good. We do not become faithful to the human identity by carving out a singular existence of self-sufficiency. We become faithful by becoming vulnerable to being affected by love, especially the love of God.

Who Are We, Anyway? The Moral Life and Our Human Identity

Allowing God to affect us with His love is the key to overcoming the temptations to the evils of selfishness, gossip, and pornography, as well as all other vices. Being good is grounded in who we are. We cannot identify who we are unless we answer the question about the meaning of life, where we come from, and where we are going. I have come to describe the human identity in the following way: We are loved-nothings. This simply means that if God did not love us, we would not exist. In other words, our existence is not *necessary* for the continuation of the universe. In fact, creation could get along quite nicely without us. The heavens, the environment, and all living things would suffer no loss if we were not here. We are, however, quite dependent upon creation. Driven by the power of our "fat relentless egos," we look upon ourselves as indispensable to the created world when we, in fact, are not.

If we are not necessary, then why do we exist? Faith and revelation tell us the only possible answer. We exist because God loves us. If God didn't love us, we would not be here. This is an astoundingly liberating revelation. We are not needed, but *desired*. Who would not prefer to be desired, to be wanted simply for being oneself? In fact, our falling in love with one another hints at the divine romance between God and ourselves. That is where our joy comes from: We find another who has already found us. We thrive on being loved for who we are. Like the kind of beloved we all crave, God loves us "just because."

This is the only satisfying answer for the human heart. If love is tied to an accidental gift or talent I possess, then I am secretly downcast. I wonder, "Will you still love me if I am not slim, musically talented, a good cook, or funny?" This is our secret fear of inadequacy rearing its ugly head. We are told through faith that God has no such conditions tied to His love of us, and we hope, with God's grace, to gift our friends and spouses with that kind of unqualified love as well. In embracing our identity as loved-nothings, we find the key to a moral life worth living. To be a loved-nothing is to live with the awareness that we exist because we are loved, but that this love is a gift, not a necessity.

Since we live in the tension of being loved-nothings, we sometimes emphasize one pole of this identity over the other. We can be guilty at times of thinking we are only "loved" or only "nothing." Concentrating only on the *loved* side of our identity distorts reality and leads to attitudes and actions of pride ("I am everything, I am special, I am loved by God"). To focus on being loved is good, but, without an awareness of the rest of our human identity, our moral life becomes too self-centered.

Alternately, ruminating about the *nothing* side of our identity can lead us to slide into despair or self-hate. This equally distorts reality. Yes, we are not *necessary*, but we are *loved*! If we focus simply upon the thought that we do not *have* to exist, if we peer into that darkness for too long, we are left feeling alone and hopeless. If, on the other hand, we live in the awareness that God loves us and that we are wanted freely by God, we are led to live a life not of pride or despair but of humble gratitude — a life of worship.

All sin arises from thinking either that we are everything or that we are nothing. When I act out of these incomplete and distorted visions of the human identity instead of out of the creative tension of being a loved-nothing, I sin. To note that is to simply acknowledge that when we sin, we are being unfaithful to the human identity, unfaithful to the fact that we are loved-nothings. The interesting life is life in the hyphen, lived in the tension between *being* loved and being nothing. Life is an undeserved gift from God's love. Living gratefully in this tension assists us in avoiding the extremes of thinking either "I am everything" or "I am nothing."

Another related tension that can leave us frustrated and choosing between extremes is the one between love of self and love of neighbor. The temptation is to think only of ourselves ("I am everything" — pride) or to think only of others by belit- tling ourselves ("I am nothing" — despair). Either way we are being unfaithful to the commandment of Christ, "[L]ove your neighbor as yourself" (Mt 19:19). Christ did not say to love one's neighbor *more* than self or *less* than self, but *as* oneself. Living in the tension of being *freely* loved into life, without going to the extremes of pride or despair, is the ingredient for an interesting life. I know how to be selfish, and I know how to give in to despair and self-hate. But how do I love God, neigh- bor, and self in a balanced way, in the "hyphen"? The Chris- tian life is an adventure into that mystery. And we would make better progress into that mysterious living if we could stop being afraid, stop clinging to self or others only and cling to God. *In God* we can know reality *as love of self and neighbor.* This is what Paul means when he teaches, "I have been crucified with Christ; yet I live, no longer I, but Christ lives in me; insofar as I now live in the flesh, I live by faith in the Son of God who has loved me and given himself up for me" (Gal 2:19-20). We do not cope all alone with human temptations to despairingly hate the self or pridefully love the self. We cope in Christ. He assists us, through the power of the indwelling Spirit, to not make decisions out of either pride or despair. And this Spirit is stirred and we allow it to grasp us through the preeminent act of worship. We are called away from the *emptiness* of gossip, pornography, and all selfish behaviors because we are meant to live *fully* in Christ. As we focus our affections on the one who is worthy of our love — Jesus Christ — instead of on ourselves in either pride or despair, we live the good life. Our life in Christ is what will complete us, and in that living we will find our heart's desire. In allowing ourselves to be grasped by God, we rise to worship and adore Him.

2

Worship and the Virtue of Listening

We Become What We Love

How does worship assist us in forming moral character and staying faithful to our identity as loved-nothings? Through the Church's public worship, believers seek to adore the Father through remembering in the Spirit the mystery of Christ's life, death, and resurrection. It is a collective act of adoring, recalling, and communing. Through worship we open ourselves to be acted upon by God and we give thanks to God for creating, sustaining, and reconciling us to Himself after we have sinned. To worship in the Eucharistic liturgy is to encounter Christ sacramentally and seek communion with Him in all His goodness. Recall that we become what we love. As we worship God in the representation of Christ's sacrifice on the cross, the giving of Himself to the Father in love, we too wish to conform to this mysterious self-giving. In the Mass we listen deeply to Christ in word and sacrament and then offer ourselves to God in imitation of Christ's self-offering. By participating in this act of worship, we begin to take on the mind of Christ. We become more and more Christian. As a result we endeavor to think and make decisions not out of pride, despair, or fear, but out of the knowledge that God freely loves us. The ethical question around the experience of regular worship becomes, "How ought one live who is so loved?" The disposition and behavior of a loved-nothing is aligned and conformed to the disposition and behavior of Christ. We want to be affected by Christ and all that Christ heard from the Father. Being affected in this way is what forms a Christian character and conscience.

Christians long to be changed by the presence of the loving God. For example, married people make decisions differently than single people because they have been changed by the one they love. It is impossible, according to the nature of Christian marriage, to successfully live a single life when one is married. When deliberating over specific actions, spouses must listen to one another and, in doing so, become sensitive to the dignity of the other in order to choose actions which are responsive to mutual needs. This kind of responsiveness can be attained because the beloved and his or her spouse are in communion. The mind is altered after communion, be it with God or spouse. In a very real sense, the spouse takes on the mind of his or her beloved. In situations demanding moral decisions, the spouse muses, "What is best for my spouse in this situation?" We *become* our beloved. And so it is for Christians, that in our worship we take on the mind of Christ and begin to think and act as Christ would. Christians come to make decisions differently than before conversion because they too have been changed by the one they love — God.

I remember an incident in my own life that convinced me of this truth. Some time ago, while my wife was away with our two boys and I was working very hard on a teaching project, the doorbell rang. I reluctantly got up from my desk, answered the door, and saw Charlie, my neighbor, there. The last thing I wanted at that moment was to be hospitable. I wanted to go back to my desk and finish my writing project.

"Hi, Charlie," I said. "What's up?"

"Oh nothing," he smiled, "'just wanted to know how you've been."

"I'm fine," I said. "Good to see you." After a few more pleasantries were exchanged, I excused myself with, "Well, I have to get back to work now."

Charlie smiled, said goodbye cheerfully, and turned to walk home. I closed the door and was walking back toward the kitchen when Marianne's face appeared in my mind. I suddenly knew that she would not have kept a visitor on the porch or been so hasty in dismissing him. Beyond this, I knew that Charlie was alone like me, since his family was traveling. Why not invite him in? Marianne would have done so. I quickly turned back, stepped onto the porch, and called out to him. When he returned I asked, "Why don't you come over and we'll have dinner?" His face brightened. "I'll grab the beer."

That was one of the happiest days of my life. Charlie's visit was pleasurable and we had some good laughs, but my happiness flowed not from that visit but from the realization that I really must love my wife because I had become her. Marianne is hospitable and generous, and seeing her face in my mind reminded me of my desire to be one with her in all things, especially virtue. I had become her, but at the same time I had become more myself than I had ever been before. This is what communion with the one you love accomplishes: union with the beloved within a sure self-knowledge. Desiring and achieving union with the beloved without losing the self is one of the most ancient truths and experiences of Christian living. We can achieve oneness with God without becoming God and losing self-awareness. And we can achieve oneness with others in a like manner. In fact, this is what ecstasy is: to be one with another and still know it.

Loving and paying attention to one's spouse is a most noble endeavor, next to loving and paying attention to God. We can become less than noble, however, if we pay attention to things of lesser dignity. I remember a time of great embarrassment when what I had been paying attention to became all too clear to others and myself. One day a seminarian came into my office and was discussing his summer parish assignment which he had received from the bishop. He named the parish he had been assigned to, and I automatically reacted negatively: "Oh, God bless you," I said, "that place is dead." He immediately responded with disappointment. "*You're* not one of *those* people, are you?"

I knew instinctively who he was referring to when saying "*those* people." They are the kinds of people who listen to gossip and take it at face value, the kinds who unreflectively agree when others belittle a parish or a pastor. I didn't think I was "one of *those* people" up until that point, but I was. The student began to tell me stories of holiness in that so-called "dead parish" that would make anyone proud to be a part of its formative liturgies and substantive catechesis. By attending to sources beneath my dignity — gossip — I had become someone who judges on hearsay and superficialities. It was painful to learn that I had paid attention to such trivia and that my character had been formed accordingly.

Conforming to Christ

Just as in marriage, becoming what we love is the dynamic heart of the moral formation that occurs in worship. Unlike marriage, however, where the focus of love is the spouse, in worship we are focused upon God. I do not worship my spouse; I worship God. But I do love my spouse and I do love God within my worship. My mind and heart are conformed to both my spouse and God, and in a real way I am becoming the good that I love in them.

The purpose of a Catholic parish is for its members to become and exhibit what is good in God, through regular worship. Our parishes should be distinguished by marks of God's goodness and holiness. "[T]he fruit of the Spirit is love, joy, peace, patience, kindness, generosity, faithfulness, gentleness, self-control. . . . Now those who belong to Christ . . . have crucified their flesh with its passion and desires. If we live in the Spirit, let us also follow the Spirit" (Gal 5:22-25). If these virtues mark our lives, we know that our minds and hearts have adhered to Christ in worship. Paul specifies this kind of moral formation in his letter to the Romans.

> I urge you . . . by the mercies of God, to offer your bodies as a living sacrifice, holy and pleasing to God, your spiritual worship. Do not conform yourselves to this age but be transformed by the renewal of your mind, that you may discern what is the will of God, what is good and pleasing and perfect (Rom 12:1-2).

Once we have conformed to Christ, we will know what is good.

Paul advises us to renew our minds and not conform to this age. Wisdom about what is right and wrong is given by God *after* a community trusts and gives itself over to God in worship. Moral wisdom is the fruit of worship, of trusting God enough to yield our minds over to Him so they might be transformed by the Spirit who is truth (see Jn 16:13). Once we enter into communion with God through the sacramental life, we are empowered to know the good and listen to the conscience in its judgment.[6] After we are in communion we know what to do. This is what happened to me in the incident with my neighbor which I described above. Only after I was in communion with Marianne could I see what was good and right and then judge what action should be taken. My hospitality was a new vision and a new behavior empowered by my relationship with my wife. And so, if a certain moral teaching appears wrong or difficult for us, perhaps we should check our worship to see if it is authentic. Are we listening to, communing with, and being conformed to "this age" (Rom 12:2), as Paul warned against, or are we attending to authentic sources of faith formation?

This knowledge of what to do morally is not infallible, nor does it automatically follow after the reception of Christ in the sacraments. Moral wisdom is the result of many years of gradually having the mind transformed by the Spirit. We know that the Church's moral law is helpful in naming what is good because we believe that men and women who were conformed to Christ over a long period originally articulated it. The Church's moral law is the fruit of the worshiping mind. The moral law. then. is to be an assistant to us as we discern right and wrong behavior in the concrete aspects of our lives. If we listen to the truths within moral law, and worship the living God in Christ's paschal mystery, there will be reasonable grounds for moral certainty in our decisions.

How does a mind that is conformed to Christ make moral judgments? When I say "mind," I am referring to our conscience — the conscience, formed by faith, is our mind acting to judge right and wrong. The conscience is not simply intuition or guilt feelings, but a judging mind filled with a knowledge of God that comes through love. It is important to remember that the conscience is being formed whether we are aware of it or not. For example, when we are little children we learn what is right and wrong by watching the behavior of our parents. What parent would not be embarrassed upon hearing his child say, "But Daddy, you said that word yesterday when you were angry," after correcting his son or daughter's rude language? If caught like this, some parents will excuse themselves by invoking the special rights of adulthood: "Yes, I said that, but that is an adult word." Perhaps this perpetual rationalization by adults is how the word "adult" became synonymous with "immoral" (as in "adult" movies, books, entertainment, etc.). Robert Coles teaches us that:

> The most persuasive moral teaching we adults do is by example: the witness of our lives, our ways of being with others and of speaking to them and getting on with them — all of that taken in slowly, cumulatively, by our sons and daughters. . . . To be sure other sources can count a great deal. . . . But in the long run of a child's life, the unselfconscious moments that are what we think of simply as the unfolding events of the day and the week turn out to be the really powerful and persuasive times, morally.[7]

If the conscience is our love-imbued mind making moral judgments, then it is hungry for direction. The judgment of conscience is not a special word implanted by God that circumvents our minds. No, we learn right and wrong as a result of being immersed in the lives of those with whom we have communion. Since the parent is the most vital presence in a child's life, his or her mind is riveted upon the parent's every move and word. In this, the child's conscience is being formed.

But in fact, some of our childhood formation needs to be corrected well into adulthood. Many of us, for example, have listened to people tell stories about being yelled at by the priest in the confessional and never returning to celebrate that sacrament. Later, we come to find out that the incident happened when the person was twelve years old, but the person continues to tell that story and be formed by that experience now, at fifty years old. Childhood experiences are formative but not absolutely definitive. Certainly, by the time we are adults, we can see that the Church and its ministry are bigger than any one priest and his rude behavior. As adults, we can change and grow and come to new insights regarding what is right or wrong. In other words, the conscience can always resume its search for the morally true and good.

Accordingly, when we grow into adulthood, our minds are no longer riveted upon our parents. Indeed, the conscience is formed not just during childhood — we continue to form our conscience until we die. Moral conversion is always a possibility and in most cases a necessity. When speaking before groups of adults, I regularly meet persons who tell me that I won't be able to teach them anything because they are "set in their ways." It is good to be set in one's ways if one's ways are Christ's ways, meaning that one is already thinking and choosing out of a mind affected by Christ and out of virtues formed by discipleship. If, however, it means that bad habits rule me and nothing and no one is going to move me away from these habits, that is not good. The moral life is not static or set in concrete. It is a living response to the truth as the mind perceives it and the Spirit empowers it to be lived out. There is stability in the moral life, but it is the stability of a moral character that has become defined by loving those things that are worthy to be loved. I have enjoyed meditating upon the story of the raising of Lazarus (see Jn 11) as a metaphor for the awakening of a conscience that is set in its ways. If Christ can raise the dead with His voice, Christ's voice can certainly penetrate the dead conscience and stir it back to a life of seeking what is good, true, and beautiful. The formation of conscience, by regularly and intentionally attending to Christ, is vital for the renewal of personal and parish moral living.

Listening

My mother gave me a great insight into the structure of conscience formation on the day that I announced to her my plans to get married. We were having lunch and discussing various things when I suddenly blurted out that I was going to ask Marianne to marry me. She was quite calm about my dramatic announcement. She smiled and said, "I knew you were going to marry her, as you never treated any other woman with such respect." Leave it to a parent to spoil a surprise by continuing to know you so well that little is surprising! Nevertheless, I thought this was a good time to ask for my mother's advice on marriage. After seven children and fifteen grandchildren, she must have much to teach. I asked, "Mom, what advice would you give me about marriage?" She took a sip of tea and said, "Pay attention." That was it. She distilled more than thirty years of marriage into two words. I must admit I was disappointed when she shared what at first appeared to be meager knowledge — only two words! I thought that she must not believe I really wanted to know her wisdom about the secrets of being married. I wanted more, but she was already finished with the lesson and had moved on to other subjects.

Now, from my current perspective from over a decade of being married, I see that her answer was a brilliant distillation of the essence of marriage and love itself. If we want to have communion with our spouse, then we must steady our gaze and work at listening to our beloved so that nothing can come between us, distract us, or tempt us to forget that we are coming to be holy primarily in that love. Similarly, in moral formation the conscience needs to fix upon God and attend only to his voice. The Second Vatican Council described the conscience as the voice of God: "Its voice, ever calling him to love and to do what is good and to avoid evil, tells him inwardly at the right moment: do this, shun that. . . . His conscience is man's most secret core, and his sanctuary. There he is alone with God whose voice echoes in his depths."[8] If the conscience does not attend to God in prayer, Scripture, worship, and doctrine, it may remain unfamiliar with God's voice. It may not recognize the divine voice and remain ignorant of what is good.

This concept of losing the ability to hear God's voice came clear to me through an experience in my marriage. Early in the marriage I was completing my doctoral studies and was obsessed with doing so within an aggressive, self-determined timetable. That schedule meant an incredible amount of study on top of a teaching position and being a husband and father. Needless to say, I didn't see much of my wife, and since she liked the idea of being married and staying faithful to her vow to "love until death," she developed a scheme to save our fledgling marriage. She wanted us to share happy hour together daily at 5:00 p.m. Being an achievement-centered person, I of course balked at her plan and saw it as something that would eat into my precious study time, but she was adamant that we try it.

I was not thrilled with this new plan, but since she was very determined to have me cooperate, I complied. Note that this attitude of reluctant compliance is very important. The first day was not a festive party; I felt I *had* to be home at 5:00 p.m. to sit with Marianne and eat snacks and drink cocktails. Admitting that I resisted what I now see clearly as such a delightful proposal proves how far off track my life had become, how narrow- and single-minded I was. Now, after ten years of enjoying cocktails and pretzels with my wife at 5:00 p.m., I can't imagine being anywhere else at that time. What then seemed like a burden is now quite pleasant. Through this simple commitment of time alone, among other activities, we have created a very good marriage. During those happy hours, I have come to appreciate how important it is to listen to one's beloved, to simply be together, and attend to each other's heart. If it weren't for my wife calling me back to our marriage, I would eventually have lost the ability to listen to her voice. Analogically, this is what can happen to our conscience. We can become too focused on voices other than Christ's. We can come to listen exclusively to the voices of popular culture, academic culture, or professional interests rather than the voice of Christ. What love relationship is at the core of our conscience? Whatever we have placed there deeply affects how we discern right and wrong.

In desiring to form a Christian conscience, we may at first resist the voice of Christ, just as I resisted Marianne's voice and wanted to remain fixated upon my professional life. This ability to resist Christ's invitation is why we need the tools of the ascetical life. In the ascetical life, a relationship with God and others is promoted and the "fat relentless ego"[9] is de-centered. In the disciplines of prayer, spiritual reading, and mortification (denying the self needless things), we will soon seek out Christ's voice, long for its clarity, wisdom, and simplicity, and revel in being in his presence. When my wife called me to happy hour, she was structuring a time for us to deny ourselves and come into a listening relationship with each other. In the same way, the ascetical and spiritual disciplines of prayer, spiritual reading, and mortification will bear their fruits: the desire to listen to Christ in the conscience.

The discipline I needed to learn, then, was very concrete: listen to my wife and stop fixating on my voice alone. It involved a place (our deck in our backyard), tools to facilitate listening and conversation (beverages, snacks), and a specific time each day. Just as I resisted what now seems like an irresistible invitation from my wife to "come and spend time being with me," so too we can resist the same invitation from God. It is even easier to resist God (since snacks and drinks are usually not provided!). How is it that we can resist an invitation that has as its end our heart's fulfillment? Generally, the answer to this question is the mystery of sin and evil. Such successful resistance comes as a result of years of egocentric choices.

After a youth ministry class I was conducting a few years ago, a boy came up to me to speak in private. He was very interested in knowing Jesus more but, predictably, he was focused upon what a relationship with Christ would cost him. His first question to me was whether he would have to stop smoking marijuana in order to follow Christ. What was he going to have to give up in order to know Jesus better? This is the question of the ego, the unattached self seeking to remain so. If we wish to "take on the mind of Christ" (1 Cor 2:16) and live out of a conscience that really does "know with" Christ (*con* = with, *science* = knowledge), we need to discipline the ego to accept that the real self is not annihilated when it comes into union with Christ. Only selfishness is destroyed by communion with Christ. When we resist moral conversion, often it is because we think we are alone and we will not be able to make choices on our own again. We, however, are not alone. We will be able to make choices, but after conversion to Christ they will not arise, overall, from the isolated ego but with and in Christ.

In describing the meaning of the human person, the French Catholic philosopher Gabriel Marcel once said, "the deepest part of me is another," meaning that at our core we are a *relationship*, not simply a *self*. In other words, I am nothing without you. All our loves mirror this metaphysical truth. The heart of *being* is relatedness, and in order to make morally good choices, all our dispositions, virtues, and actions must reverence this unchangeable reality. When I resist following my conscience, initially I do so because I feel as if I am losing my self, as if my self is being killed. Often there is such a dramatic resistance to moral conversion because we do not realize that being good *is* a killing of *something* — but it is the death of something that is not worth keeping. Moral conversion means killing our selfishness. But if most of our actions and thoughts have been selfish, that is much indeed! The selfish self may in fact be the only self one has ever known, thus in moral conversion it may indeed feel as if our entire self is being destroyed.

It is understandable that we initially inquire about what we are going to lose when putting on the mind of Christ. But after a while, and it could be a long while because of our stubbornness and God's incredibly gentle yet persuasive call, we have to decide out of what center of reality we will live, the "I" or the "We"? The high-school boy who clung to an identity as a marijuana smoker soon came to realize that in Christ new and lasting identities are formed. I came to see that I lost nothing important in sharing happy hour with my wife, just the anxiety and depression of building a world that revolved only around me. The first step is to *desire* to have a conscience that listens to Christ. No, actually, the first step is to *pray for the desire* to want such a conscience, and then seek the structure necessary to sustain a life of listening to Christ.

In this chapter I pointed to the centrality of three vital areas in preparing oneself to form a Christian conscience. First, we should grow in joyful awareness of the formative value of worship. Second, listening to who or what we love is what forms us. And finally, correcting our years of listening to less ennobling objects of love (i.e., self alone or segments of popular culture) will take discipline. The need for asceticism is vital because we have become a certain kind of person in listening to anemic formation sources and now we need to struggle away from them. Some will struggle harder and longer than others, but struggle we must if we have loved beneath our dignity. I will say more about the importance of asceticism in the next chapter, as I explore the concrete elements of forming the Christian conscience.

3

Forming a Christian Conscience

n forming a Christian conscience, our minds become immersed in the meaning of our baptismal identity. It is by this identity that we live as Christians. Certainly, the entire world is God's and all peoples deserve our respect for their inherent human dignity, but it seems impossible for us to be "generically" human. We need a community, a tradition out of which we consciously draw the meaning of our lives. For those who have encountered Christ and who follow Him by the force of His truth and beauty, the Church becomes this tradition of life. As disciples, we turn toward the Church in all its riotous diversity and development, and in all its essential consistency, in order to form our consciences.[10] We do not turn exclusively to the Church to attend to moral truth, as this truth is also found beyond the Church, but as Catholics we do turn to the Church primarily and intentionally. And turning our minds to Church doctrine for the formation of conscience is not the same as turning our minds off. Our minds need to be fully, personally engaged in the appropriation of the truth of moral doctrine. Sin, weakness, and error are certainly present within Church leaders and members.[11] In acknowledging these limitations, we see that we need to form our minds in both the rigors of critical thinking and in the ascetical regimen of devotion to Christ — a mindless obedience to institutional leaders, or to institutions in general, will not serve the truth.

There is, however, no disembodied Christ simply waiting in abeyance to be summoned at will. The only Christ I know has come to me through the Church, a Church that has become institutionalized. This Church can be reformed and renewed but it does have a relative stability of doctrine, ritual, and moral norms. As an institution, the Church can descend into institutionalism, which primarily secures and promotes the organization as an end in itself. This, of course, would be self-defeating for the Church, as it exists to be on a mission and to serve those beyond itself. Some Catholics have left organized religion because of their experience of perceived institutionalism, wherein parishes or dioceses have preserved the organization at the expense of charity toward individuals. On Sundays, instead of being formed by attending public worship, these disaffected Catholics go for a walk in the woods or spend time in quiet contemplation at home. This is an old American tradition actually, individualists that we are. But if significant numbers no longer attend public worship, this could signal a disturbance that is deeper than simple American individualism. Institutionalism and individualism are the two extreme poles we need to avoid. Neither forms a well-ordered conscience. The celebration of the Eucharist, however, is the activity that secures the Christ-like mind.

The Eucharist and Formation

Worshiping at the Eucharist is vital because it is the place where Christ *promised* to meet us. The Eucharist brings the community into an encounter with Christ. The Mass, in its ritual action, is Christ's "pledge . . . in order never to depart from his own and to make us sharers in his Passover."[12] In the Mass we gather around the table to consume the Body and Blood of Christ and to immerse ourselves in the Word of God. In this gathering, we are formed as Catholics. Of course, one can experience mystical delight in a prayerful walk in the woods or in prayer at home. And this kind of private prayer, which draws on the indwelling of the Holy Spirit, should be encouraged and practiced. Christ did not promise, however, to meet us *as Church* in the redwoods, but in the bread and wine and the Word proclaimed. He is there waiting for us, calling us into intimacy, and strengthening us for service to the needy. I have nothing against either walking in the woods or private prayer, but I have always thought they were incomplete. Recently, as I drove to meet Marianne for dinner at a restaurant, I found out why.

What would happen, I imagined, if instead of going to meet my wife I decided to go for a walk in the woods and *think* about her. Sure, I would have her on my mind as I walked, but our promise to each other was to meet in the restaurant. If I went to the restaurant, I could *really* encounter her instead of just *thinking* about her in the woods. It is pleasant to think about God (meditation) and desirable to converse with God privately (prayer), but Christ promised His community that when we remember Him in the Eucharist He will be present sacramentally (public worship). When I arrived at the restaurant, I noticed that it was arranged in order to facilitate intimacy between my wife and me. There were candles, music, wine, food, and an environment that affirmed and supported our meeting. The environment was well-suited to facilitate conversation with Marianne, to get to know her through such dialogue. Analogically, the only difference between the restaurant and Sunday worship is that at Sunday worship we are all giving ourselves to and communicating with the same object of our love, God. In the Mass, where bread, wine, candles, and music facilitate our concentration upon the beloved, we meet our heart's desire in the breaking of the bread. All analogies suffer, but I would rather be in that restaurant to meet Marianne as promised, and in that church with fellow Catholics as Mass begins in order to encounter Christ, than simply to be alone in the woods with my private thoughts.

Our baptismal identity is communal and transcendent, and the conscience becomes clear and strong in its judgments as we become clear and strong in our baptismal identities. "Showing up" at Mass on Sunday is, at minimum, an action that keeps the lines of communication open between God, Church, and self. Just showing up is not the goal, of course, but it does at least imply that one is aware of a communal identity, and this is the first step in the formation of a Catholic conscience. There is also the *quality* of one's presence that needs to be addressed.

On a recent visit with my friend Helen and her husband, John, I arrived at their home before John came in from work. While waiting for him to arrive, Helen and I visited in the living room. Suddenly we heard the kitchen door open and she excused herself to go and meet John at the door. They did not return immediately. I could hear them having "words" in the kitchen. At one point Helen said, "You are an hour late," and John responded, "Well, I came home, didn't I?" Of course, it is *vital*, at minimum, to *show up* at the place or gathering where you are to meet someone. We know, however, that actually encountering someone and having communion with that person takes more self-exertion than simply appearing physically in the same space as the other person. It is good to show up, but more is necessary. The "more necessary" involves that maternal advice I received upon announcing my plans to get married: "Pay attention." The question of forming a Christian conscience involves becoming a Christian person, and that means paying attention to that which Christians love.

What is it that Christians love? Obviously the primary object of our love is God in Christ. To pay attention to Christ is to adhere to the *sources* and *experiences* that manifest His presence. First among these is the Church. Paying attention to the Church is a complex process of listening and adhering and desiring. The Church is such an intricate object of love that we cannot simply reduce it to one's pastor, or the pope, or even the fellowship of one's local parish. The Church includes all these things, but it is also manifested in a culture — in a way of life that orders values and calls one to express those values through acquiring certain dispositions and behaviors. This is not to say, however, that the Church is some ephemeral haze that cannot be accessed concretely. It is entered into through the local community, but even as it encompasses the local, it also facilitates a relationship with the Church as a whole — the Universal Church. By this I simply mean that being Catholic identifies one with a tradition that is both beyond and inclusive of one's local church, parish, and national affiliation. When we pay attention to our ecclesial identity, we are acknowledging our connectedness to a community of people stretching back in time, through the present, and into eternity.

Virtues or Rules?

Within this community we encounter Christ in the Word, in the sacraments, and in the practice of the virtues. In practicing the moral and theological virtues, we are conformed to an end that is nothing other than the goal of human life: holiness. Virtue is encompassed in affectivity; one has to desire to be good, but often one practices virtue in simply *knowing* that such behavior is correct. There may be times when practicing a virtue yields no measurable feeling per se.

For instance, once Marianne and I decided to attempt reconciliation with a longtime friend from whom we had been recently estranged. We wanted to offer hospitality and say that whatever wounds we had caused one another were not bigger than the friendship itself. We decided to attempt this reconciliation within a party, so we invited several friends over to watch an Ohio State-Notre Dame football game on TV. When our estranged friend arrived, it was a bit uncomfortable; that old spontaneity and give and take were missing. Conversation was strained, so Marianne and I decided to concentrate on the food and the game. The evening went slowly, and immediately upon the game's conclusion our friend thanked us and left. We have never seen him again formally. Nor did he ever reciprocate with an invitation to his house. Later Marianne and I reflected upon this incident and felt as though we had failed. Yes, it seems we had failed in our attempt to resurrect a friendship, but we took solace in noting that we did the right thing. The party yielded no good feelings in anyone. No new intimacy arose from the invitation we extended, but it was the right thing to do. In other words, by inviting our friend to our house we willed the good; we practiced the virtue of hospitality, and that in itself was a worthwhile exercise for us and for our friend.

Virtues are consistent patterns of thought, feeling, and behavior that direct the person to a good end (see Col 3:12-17). For the Christian these virtues are completed in the gifts of the Holy Spirit, which possess the virtuous person and direct him or her not simply to the moral good but to God. For Christians, it is a goal in moral living to live out the virtues, as opposed to rules. Moral rules are for children and adult moral emergencies. By this I mean that rules can arise within the conscience and be valuable during times of temptation and act as reminders of what is basic to being a good person. As we grow older and more mature, however, we seek to get behind the rules and understand their truths — the *truths* of rules become incorporated into our character and assist in forming a life of virtue. It is the *truths* of moral rules and principles that our minds adhere to and think out of in ethical discernment. Without understanding the truths behind the moral rules, we will eventually discard the rules themselves as irrelevant, or we will come to blindly obey rules as our only way to be guided.

For the Catholic, the conscience needs to be nurtured by the truth and not simply by the formulated rules.

The Moral Truth

This leads me to the eternal question: What is truth? The general answer is, of course, that God is truth. The depth of the truth of God is the mystery we are to plumb for eternity. It is a more than satisfying journey. It is a journey we take with our head and heart, with and among other persons. And this journey is *in God*, and therefore is infinitely satisfying for us. We begin to taste that journey before death as we respond to grace and moral truth. Recognizing the moral truth is vital for our growth in virtue, and so it is necessary to situate ourselves within that community which fosters our moral destiny in God — the Church. The Church trains us to recognize the truth. It does so by immersing us in the stories and truths of Christ's life and teachings. "The more that Christians internalize the Christian story, the more they will be able to grasp the authentic values in each situation and the appropriateness of their actions."[13] In other words, the Church forms us to take on the mind of Christ, who is truth. The moral truth is recognized as a fruit of knowing Christ. Dissatisfaction with one's life may be an invitation to look harder at the values present there and see if the moral truth is at its heart or if one's life is based only upon partial truths, such as success alone, money alone, power alone, pride alone, etc. The moral truth involves us in what is good for us as *Christian* persons, not simply as cultural citizens or talented professionals. The moral truth is about action that is real for us who have been grasped by the love of God in Christ. In the context of one's Christian identity, the moral question becomes, "Can this behavior I am contemplating be integrated into the values of the Gospel?"

All that is authentically human is taken up into, affirmed, and truly known in all that is authentically Christian. In this way, our lives become a metaphor for the incarnation of God.

Through our graced response to our baptismal identities, we mirror what God did in Christ and wants to do in us in a different yet real way: join us to Himself. The Christian moral life is one that slowly integrates a person's character and behavior into the divine life. What is morally true is that which can abide with and in God. We know what kind of action and character that truth is by conforming our minds to the mind of Christ, as I discussed previously. We conform our minds to Christ by loving Him in word, sacrament, and service to the poor. As Pope John Paul II has said:

> It is the heart converted to the Lord and to the love of what is good which is really the source of true judgments of conscience. Indeed, in order to "prove what is the will of God, what is good, and acceptable and perfect" (Rom 12:2), knowledge of God's law in general is certainly necessary but not sufficient: what is essential is a sort of connaturality between man and the true good. Such a connaturality is rooted in and develops through the virtuous attitudes of the individual himself: prudence and the other cardinal virtues, and even before these the theological virtues of faith, hope, and charity. This is the meaning of Jesus' saying: "He who does what is true comes to the light" (Jn 3:21).[14]

The kind of knowing which the pope calls "connatural" grasps the truth in an intuitive way. It is a kind of deep knowing, a "knowing that I know." This kind of knowing is the result of loving God and what is good. It is the fruit of thinking out of love. And it is love that forms the mind to grasp what is morally true. In the baptismal life we are "not just moved by reason but by God."[15] By loving Christ, by communing with

Him, we become certain kinds of persons who grow to trust our love-imbued reasoning in its judgments of right and wrong. In fact, as we grow in holiness, we begin to live out of that which is *within us* more than that which has been *given to us* in principle and rules.

I once met a man, Tom, who discovered the truth of his moral life only by first attending to the presence of Christ in his life. He refers to his moral conversion as "harvest day," tracing his conversion to seeds planted by his parents in their spare but authentic moral teachings. Tom was a successful businessman who owned a company that sold heavy machinery repair and replacement parts. His business was flourishing until some poor investments started to siphon off too much capital. Tom was tempted to steal money to shore up the business. One day, however, he recalled his father's voice from childhood repeating the Ten Commandments. The recollection of the commandment "Thou shalt not steal" invited him to visit a nearby church during his lunch hour. As he entered the church, a place he had not visited for decades, he reported feeling such an overwhelming presence of love that he sat down in a pew and stayed for an hour. During that hour he looked at the paintings on the wall, the statues, the crucifix, and the tabernacle. He told me that "the place was holy; it made me feel peaceful." After that day he began to go to Mass again. One month passed and through tears he celebrated the Sacrament of Reconciliation for the first time in thirty years. Since then he attends worship regularly. "I couldn't think of stealing any money today, even though morality cost me dearly [financially]."

The seeds to his moral renewal were planted in his childhood but came to full bloom by attending to Christ in the midst of a worshiping community. After a time of communing with Christ in the assembly, he came to see the moral truth. Over the months since his initial visit to the downtown church, he conversed with other Catholic laypersons as well as priests.

The community advised him morally and spiritually. These fellow believers even supported Tom financially as his business collapsed and he had to build a new professional life. There is a cost to being good; but, in a real Christian community, the burden of that cost is to be shared by the parish to the extent that virtue will allow. As St. Paul teaches, "Bear one another's burdens, and so you will fulfill the law of Christ. . . . Let us not grow tired of doing good, for in due time we shall reap our harvest, if we do not give up" (Gal 6:2, 9).

God calls us to repent in a way that fits our personalities and life circumstances. Not everyone will come to God by recalling the Ten Commandments and entering a sacred place. Some will be called at art galleries or in hospitals or at home. Coming to the parish, however, is what is universal to all a Christian moral conversions. One cannot become good *as a Christian* without the Church. *How* God finds us and *how* God leads us is unique to who we are. *That* God invites us to the community of faith and moral truth is a universal call. In this community we learn the practices of moral and spiritual living. To these I now turn.

Spiritual and Moral Training

Some are blind to the moral truth because they have lived so long in sin that they mistake the sinful life for the good life. When grace fills us, we have the opportunity to see clearly and leave the dark. The process of conversion involves moving away from a sinful life and can call for ascetical practices. Asceticism is necessary when our mind has grown to love what is beneath our dignity. Over months or years of choosing wrongly, our will seeks out behavior that is immoral. Summarily, we need to learn again to love what is good. Ascetical practices and penance help us break the habits of old thinking and willing and "put on the new self" (Eph 4:24).

Some form of spiritual training or asceticism is essential for Christian conscience formation. This ascetical turn should be done in consultation with those who have already undergone its purifying effects. We can find people who have been so trained by attending to the characters of our spiritual leaders, by following the referrals of spiritual directors, or by going to where it is reasonable to assume spiritual leaders are found (i.e., monasteries, theology schools, parishioners who pray and serve the parish, etc). Being purified of the blindness that is brought on by years of sinning is not an easy transition, but staying in a state of moral blindness is an even worse suffering.

In the foremost asceticism of prayer, we enter the matrix of true moral conversion. In this kind of training — training to listen — we receive light and salvation. "As light, Christ takes away my ignorance, as my salvation he takes away my weakness."[16] To contextualize this prayerful asceticism in the parish, let us imagine a life of listening to Christ from within, a lifetime of listening to the Eucharistic "host" (Latin *hostia* = victim). As we become more and more attuned to listening to Christ as victim, we will be encouraged by Christ to listen to and be formed by other victims as well. These victims will be the community of parishioners around us, the ones that welcome or host cancer, poverty, loneliness, injustice, and the like. Christ the host is speaking to us and calling out to us to serve those who have been the victims of sin, whether their own or another's. This is why we exist in community. Attending to these victims is a strong form of asceticism and purification for a conscience that is stuck in blindness or selfish bias. Why is this so?

Limits

Most commonly, our consciences awake when our minds perceive a limit. Personal or communal failure is a powerful antidote to a life of biased self-importance. This kind of failure or limit is perceived in our own sickness or humiliations. We embrace a change of heart when we embrace our own powerlessness. Connecting limit and failure to moral conversion is simply a way of noting that at one point, through our own failures, or by living in compassion with those who are powerless, we come to see that we are not God and that that is good. After embracing this truth we turn to worship to adore God. In living a life of adoration, our own identities are clarified — this was the case with my friend Tom.

It is not only our limitations that awaken the conscience, but also joy and ecstasy. We can come to moral awareness by *reaching* our limits (suffering) or by *breaking* them (transcendence, ecstasy, and joy). Breaking our limits indicates experiences of love and joy, experiences wherein we are surprised by the presence of another. This presence enthralls us and sheds light upon how limited our vision of reality was before this meeting. It may even lead us to repent of sins and, as a result, know deeper union with the loved one, be it God, spouse, or friend. James Hanigan comments on this experience of breaking limits:

> There is the unlooked for awakening to the presence of transcendent reality in . . . life, which provokes . . . a new awareness of both the divine and the human. . . . There is the re-orientation of the self which involves [acknowledging sin] but which terminates in comfort and hope. [The moment] is neither self-provided or self-initiated, but elicited by the encounter with divine presence.[17]

Just as we are sadly surprised by our limitations and the suffering that accompanies them, so it is that we are joyfully surprised by transcendence, that gift of going beyond the self in order to have communion with God and others. This kind of joy and ecstasy affords an opportunity to form our conscience and character, just as do experiences of suffering. These joys and sufferings, however, are the extraordinary influences of formation, received as gifts from God. The ordinary formation — found in daily acts of faith, hope, and love, and service, prayer, and study — is more crucial over the long run. These ordinary, daily acts solidify our self-chosen direction and are not simply given to us.

In the clarity of our real identity, we align ourselves with the community that worships and recalls its identity daily in the One who gave Himself totally to God, even unto death. In the conversion of the conscience, there is an awakening to the holy and to the good, and a re-orientation of the self toward communion with God and others for one's own sake and the sake of the community. In other words, moral conversion, in the midst of religious devotion, awakens one to reality.

In sum, the vital aspect of Catholic moral living is the formation of conscience and character according to what we love. Moral conversion is the fruit of attending to God in love. This is so because in turning our hearts to God in adoration and worship, we are made vulnerable to receive the truth about our dignity as beloved of God, and we begin to live accordingly, in truth and with dignity.

What is most important to remember regarding a Christian moral conversion is that coming to appropriate the moral good happens in the full context of one's identity as a Spirit-led person. The secular alone will not enliven the Christian heart and may, in fact, even confuse its affections. The Spirit-led heart is to be trusted *within* a larger context of worship, Word, and work (service to others).

4

Sin and Forgiveness

n Mark 10:46-52 we read the story of blind Bartimaeus. In this story the blind man hears that Jesus is coming by and cries out to Christ for mercy (see 10:47). Others around try to quiet him. Perhaps they think that Bartimaeus is embarrassing them and himself by yelling out. But he refuses to be silent. He senses that this is his only chance to have his sight restored. Jesus calls to Bartimaeus through one of His disciples. The disciple says, "Take courage; get up, he is calling you" (Mk 10:49). Jesus asks the man what he wants and Bartimaeus replies that he wants to see. Jesus heals the man's blindness and proclaims that Bartimaeus's faith is what saved him. After receiving his sight, Bartimaeus becomes a disciple of Jesus.

Christ heals not only our bodies, but our sinful ways as well (see Mk 2:1-12). Turning from our sins and receiving new sight — a new way of viewing reality — is the fruit of living a life of faith in Christ. The moral life will awaken within us as we trust in Christ and throw our sins upon His mercy. The result of this trust will be not condemnation but regeneration.

The key to the story of Bartimaeus is in the last line of the narrative, "[Bartimaeus] followed him on the way (10:52)." The result of an encounter with Christ is the desire to follow Him through the cross to the resurrection. In a healing encounter with Christ, we come to desire a share in the life of Him Who gave us Life. The first step, however, is to cry out as Bartimaeus did, "Jesus, Son of David, have pity on me." We are to shout out to Christ, even in an embarrassing fashion if necessary, because we realize that if we do not we will be forever molded by sin rather than grace.

Without Christ we decay: We lose our sight, our mind, and our power to discern good and evil; our joy is subdued, and our world shrinks to the mindless boredom of self-concern. Sin shapes us into persons who lack empathy. We become beings who cannot see beyond the narrow confines of our own experiences. Against all of this Bartimaeus cries out, "Have pity on me!" And Christ has pity because that is who Christ is, the compassion of God among us. Cry out to Christ *from the heart* because that is where all sin starts (see Mk 7:20-23). It is the heart that must be reshaped and realigned to commune not with darkness but with the light of the world (see Jn 8:12).

Naming our need for forgiveness is crucial to moral conversion. In the infamous story of President Bill Clinton's advisor Dick Morris we read of Morris' adulterous affair. This sin was front-page news during the 1996 presidential campaign. After news of his affair was reported, Morris confessed:

> It's too simple to say it was a sexual addiction . . . saying I was sick like I had pneumonia or the mumps. . . . It's not that at all. I had, I have and I hope to be getting over a fundamental flaw in my character, a fundamental weakness in my personality, a fundamental sin, if you will. . . . I'm prone to being infatu-

ated with power and believing that the rules
don't apply to me.[18]

This is as fine a definition of sin from a secular perspective
as I have read. It is not as pithy as "Son of David, have pity on
me," but the same *crie de coeur* is present. Morris went on to
say in the newspaper article that his conversion to the truth
about himself was due to his wife's fidelity during the public
humiliation they endured. Of her he said, "She's a magnificent
woman, and she didn't in the slightest . . . deserve what happened to her."[19] Did others think she was "magnificent" in her
fidelity to this adulterer? During one of the newscasts about
the Morris scandal, it was announced that his wife had forgiven him. As a response to this announcement, the women
with whom I was watching the news conference spouted a rush
of angry words: "She's an idiot!" and "What a doormat!" Another person said later about this reaction, "My, things have
changed — today we stone the woman caught in fidelity!"
Sadly, the Morris marriage ended in divorce. Could any of us
stand the pressure of such public exposure?

I believe those in Christ could weather even such a storm,
if they had a supportive community and grounded themselves
in prayer. He who could raise the dead and give sight to the
blind can reach the consciences of married couples with His
voice. His voice summoned Lazarus and Bartimaeus to new
life and healing — it can certainly summon us to virtuous living. Just naming our sin is insufficient to a complete moral
conversion, so a second thing is also necessary: entrusting our
sin and ourselves to Christ.

In leaving patterns of sin behind and giving the moral life a
try, one wills or practices in grace the "newness of life" of
which Paul spoke (Rom 6:4). To some extent many of us enter
the moral life by living *as if* we believed the truths of Church
teaching. Since sin has bound us to its reality for so long, it can
be a struggle to enter a new way of living. This struggle to live

morally, however, will not last long. Soon, as we practice the life of virtue in faith, moral living becomes easier and we actually feel attracted to what is good — we recognize it and desire it. Consequently, we are gradually repulsed by what is evil. Nonetheless, sin has powerful effects upon us. When we live in sin, we are becoming a certain kind of person. Analogically, living a sinful life is similar to the experience of losing one's reputation. The lost reputation can stem from one past action, but one becomes identified with that act everywhere one goes. This is what happened to Dick Morris — popularly, for a time, he was known for being an adulterer, not for any other aspect of his life. Similarly, we cannot simply box our sinful choices off from the rest of who we are; those choices contribute to our identity. But we protest, "I did that sinful act in that place, during that time, yesterday, not today." Maybe so, but unless we repent, that act has entered into who we are, and even as it flowed out of us, it now creates us.

The only thing that can help sinners is the power of forgiveness. In forgiveness between persons, one incorporates the wounds inflicted upon him or her by another into a love for that person. Forgiveness acknowledges and suffers the evil inflicted, but it desires to incorporate those wounds into an ongoing relationship of love and justice. Anyone who has had a friend or a spouse knows how to forgive and hopefully how to be forgiven by the others. Without the power of forgiveness, no one could sustain relationships in any *meaningful* way because the wounds inflicted by sin would simply remain wide open. Immersing these wounds into a relationship of love is the balm that heals the wounds of sin.

Forgiveness cannot erase the scars, however. Even the resurrected Christ still bore the scars of His crucifixion wounds, testifying that sin is real, that it counts and does damage. Sin causes real changes in people's lives, but in grace victims can rise above the sin done to them. This new life, however, cannot be real unless the results of being sinned against are integrated into it and then transcended. Resurrection happens because Jesus embraced the reality of being harmed by evil; the crucifixion was real — but He embraced those evil acts against Him *with faith in the Father*. We too must know the effects of others' sins against us in faith — only this faith will see us through to forgiveness and new life.

Living in Reality

The sinner thinks that there is no objective reality, that nothing counts. This is why we hear people say things like "It was nothing; get over it." Only the one who has inflicted the wounds can make such light of them. The victim knows he was sinned against, knows it was real, and knows it will take more than the dismissive words of the perpetrator of his pain to change that reality. *Only* forgiveness will change the reality of being sinned against. As sinners, however, we tend to want nothing to count in this world; nothing regarding morality, that is. We *do* want our professional achievements to count and our sports games to count. In fact we implicitly realize that if our school grades, professional achievements, and sports scores didn't count, our participation in them would be relatively meaningless. For instance, when we go to a ball game, we expect the batter to sit down if he doesn't hit the ball after three swings or if the ball he hits is caught by the right fielder. How would we react if someone from the dugout yelled "do-over"? We would be angry. We want the actions of the batter and fielder to count because that is what makes the game interesting and worth the money paid. Actions count. If you swing three times and do not connect with the ball, you sit down. That is the reality of the game.

Why then is it difficult for us to see that if our moral behavior doesn't count, then life is meaningless? If we continue to live as if sins do not count, life will remain ultimately dull. We will feel, and in fact *be*, empty, and we will either seek out the legitimate Savior or fill our days with distractions, entertainment, or various forms of abusive and/or addictive behaviors.

In other words, we will either enter reality, or we will continue to construct a false escape route. True reality is the love and truth found in communion with God, self, and other persons. If we disrupt this, we fail as human beings. That sounds harsh, but the possibility of moral failure is vital to consider if we are to live in reality, a reality within which our free and knowledgeable choices *do* count.

Understanding sin as law-breaking is for the newborn in the faith. Sin understood as law-breaking is like Dick Morris being punished by his wife because he gave to another what rightfully was owed to her — i.e., sex. In principle this is true. But the horror of adultery is not primarily found in violations of justice but in rejecting a person, rejecting the beloved. It is her face that is rejected, her body, her soul; he promised his self, his body, his face, his person only to her. In the marriage vow, we promise to live in reality, to live in communion with the beloved and with God. To break that bond is to test the very limits of reality. The outrage of sin is not that we break a law but that we break faith.

In a legal consciousness, all one needs in order to get out of debt is to pay a fine. In a communion consciousness, one cannot *do* anything to get out of debt; one can only *receive forgiveness*. There is no other way back to reality. To live without being forgiven and without forgiving is to live a lie. It is to attempt to live outside of communion with others. This can only be done through psychic denial, rationalization, or self-deception. Needless to say, that kind of living takes a lot of work. It is easier to live in reality: to ask for forgiveness when needed and to offer it when asked. I am not suggesting that offering or asking is easy. I am simply saying that life will be authentic if forgiveness is accomplished. To be forgiven doesn't mean the wounds I caused are forgotten, and to forgive doesn't mean you think the wounds were inconsequential. Rather, the reason we forgive and are forgiven is that we acknowledge that something morally evil really happened!

Several years ago I had a teaching colleague whose personality grated against me. We shared an office for a time, but I would usually ignore her and do my work. One day she couldn't take it anymore and yelled at me, "What am I, a piece of furniture? Can't you even acknowledge me?" I immediately apologized, but didn't feel remorse, only anger. I didn't like her to begin with, and her yelling at me only made it worse. What right did she have to yell at me? We implicitly decided to hate each other. We only spoke when professionally necessary. Finally, we were given separate offices, which helped a great deal — now we could hate one another more easily by *never* speaking.

During one spring semester I was working in my office with the door ajar. This colleague's office was two doors down the hall and on the opposite side. She had her door open as well, and I heard her talking about me to one of my students. All of what she had to say about me was negative, defamatory, and false. I couldn't believe my ears. I was so angry that I went to the dean. After listening sympathetically, he told me that I had missed a step and should have first spoken directly to the teacher. I was afraid. I was afraid of my hate, my anger. I couldn't face her. What would I feel? What would I *do* to her? After a while I calmed down and went to speak to her. I was still angry, but was able to confront her and quote her directly as a result of overhearing the conversation she had with my student. She was dumbfounded. She had no idea I was in my office, able to hear her remarks. I left with a threat: "If you don't apologize to me and correct the lies you told to that student, I will report you to the dean for professional misconduct." Soon after, she apologized to me, brought the student into my office, and explained that the personal grudge she held against me was the source of her defamatory statements. I was satisfied. I thanked her, and they left. The abyss between us, however, deepened even further. I noticed that she treated me with a little more wariness, probably only because she knew she "owed me one," but there was no real breakthrough to decency in the way we treated each other.

Later that year I accepted a post at another school. On my last day of work we met each other by chance on a stairway. She was quite anxious to speak with me. Grabbing both of my shoulders and looking me right in the eyes, she said, "I cannot tell you how sorry I am for what I have I done to you. Will you please forgive me?" Now it was my turn to be dumbfounded. In that moment I realized all that I had done to her as well. I had hated her; the bad feelings I harbored against her arose whenever I saw her. Furthermore, I did not trust her, and from the first time we worked together I treated her in such a disparaging way that she had to cry out for recognition, "What am I, a piece of furniture?" Looking at her face and eyes, which I had avoided doing for several years, I thought, "No, you are not a piece of furniture; you are a person, insecure, frightened, harboring your own struggles and sins, but a person who deserves respect, not hate." I found myself blurting out, "Will you forgive me, also?" "Yes, yes, of course," she said. Taking my arm and gently guiding me over to the side of the landing where we had been standing, she whispered, "I must tell you something else."

She had a wide grin on her face and began to recount how she had an intense mystical experience of the heart of Christ. She knew now that Jesus *was* the mercy of God among us. She said, "Of course I will forgive you, out of the power of the one who has forgiven me." Her eyes began to fill with tears, and so did mine. What was happening? I wondered. Was this real? I have since come to realize that that moment was the only real encounter we had known together over our several years of working side by side. Yes, it was real, and it was the establishment of a certain level of communion with her. My relationship to her was the most painful experience I knew while at that school. But now I was truly happy because I could leave without that conflict lingering in my mind and heart. There was a peace within me.

Only forgiveness can untangle the web of evil we construct for ourselves when we live in fear and falsehood. To attempt to trace the tangle back and unravel it on one's own can be overwhelming; it is usually unproductive anyway. Our freely chosen actions, and those not so freely chosen, need to be lifted up to Christ and yielded over to his mercy. This is the kind of liberation Christ came to effect. This is why we call Him Savior. It is no accident that my colleague came to me only after her intense prayer experience. Religious faith leads to repentance. I was caught up in her repentance and saw my own guilt more clearly than before. I owned my guilt and saw how I, too, contributed to the awful working relationship we had. Grace — the presence of Christ — is like that. It spreads out to touch all who are open and draws all into communion with Christ and one another. Sin and its effects are real, but He who is the healer of sinful wounds — Jesus Christ — meets sin in grace.

Learning to See Others

It is important to note that this fellow teacher and I did not become best friends after our reconciliation. God was not giving us to one another as friends. Our needs were much more basic. In forgiveness we were simply being given to one another as fellow human beings and Christians. Friendship was nowhere near where we were. Friendship would be a second kind of grace that we might eventually receive, but finally seeing one another as *persons* was all we were called to then. Evil begins when we do not see others as persons. In this blindness (i.e., treating someone like a piece of furniture), we can ignore or attack our fellow human beings because we do not see them as worth our time. In fact, we do not see them at all.

When I was in college I lived in a house with many roommates. One Monday morning, there was a knock at the door of our house. I answered the door and there on the porch stood a girl whom I would characterize as unattractive; in fact, that was my very first thought when I saw her. At that point in my college career I was on the lookout for a girlfriend, and all fellow female collegians were reduced in my mind to their usefulness in supplying me with a date or two. In my distorted vision at that time, this girl did not measure up. "May I help you?" I asked. She explained that she was working on a project for school with one of my roommates and wondered if she could come in and wait for him to return home. "Sure," I said. "Come on in." I showed her to a chair and asked if she wanted a drink, which she declined. I excused myself and went upstairs to my room.

Apparently this was a long-term project, because each day I arrived home to find her sitting in the chair in our living room. The first day I said "hi." The second, the same. The third, I remember nodding as I passed by quickly. By the fourth day I don't even remember seeing her sitting there. She had in fact become the chair! Halfway up the stairs I stopped and thought, "What am I doing? That is a human being down there, and I should at least be pleasant to her!" If only I had integrated *that* insight into my mind and heart, I would have saved myself a lot of heartache when relating to my teaching colleague, the one who years later accused me of treating her like furniture. I went back down and began speaking to my fellow collegian. Over the months, we became friends. But at first this girl was not "useful" (not dating material) to me, so I could ignore her. Sin has its roots in this utilitarian vision of human relations. Again, we do not have to be *friends* with everyone, but we are called to respect people simply for being people and not for what they can do for us. Sin begins when we do not *see* people.

Loneliness and Moral Evil

This kind of blindness toward people can break apart any semblance of community and friendliness, leaving us terribly alone. Loneliness is a real hothouse for moral evil. People who exist in a prolonged loneliness are often the next perpetrators or victims of evil. In Genesis 2 we are told that it is not good for people to be alone. At the depths of who we are, the very core of our identity is relatedness. As I mentioned above, the French philosopher Gabriel Marcel once affirmed that "the deepest part of me is another." To live in isolation for prolonged periods of time — whether this is due to our own character flaws or to the unjust judgments against us that are held by others — is a dangerous temptation to violent rebellion. This is one reason why the Catholic Church promotes hospitality toward the poor and their empowerment toward societal participation. To remain marginalized is to tempt evil, and to be forced into marginalization is an affront to human dignity. It is no accident how citizens describe the attributes of their neighbors who are caught in criminal activity: "He was a quiet man who kept to himself." Of course he was — evil by its very nature is self-enclosed. Scott Peck once described the character of evil by saying that the person whose character is bent by evil speaks a mantra deep within himself, "Everyone must be like me, think like me, and act like me until only I exist, ruling over no one but myself."[20] That is a perfect description of hell.

Imagine a teenage boy and girl on their first date. The girl has not been on a date for quite some time. She is looking forward to this night out because she is lonely. The boy comes by her house, picks her up in his car, and they head off to a mutual friend's house for a party. They mingle together at the party for awhile and then separate in order to socialize with their own friends. The evening winds down and they find themselves riding home in the car. The boy makes small talk and the girl responds. Suddenly, he begins another line of conversation. He compliments her but then sheepishly sneaks in a criticism: "Don't take this wrong or anything, but when we were apart at the party I heard your laugh all the way into the other room. It . . . it was kind of loud. But don't worry, it's no big deal." The girl is a little confused and embarrassed. "Oh," she says, "I didn't realize." "Don't worry about it," the boy says. He continues, "Uh, just one more thing — your dress, it's a great dress, but I noticed that guys were looking at you when we walked in. It's kinda short; it's nice, don't get me wrong, but you know. . . ." The girl self-consciously shifts in her seat, pulling on her hemline. "Oh," she says.

And on it goes. Over the next couple of months of dating, the boy manages to criticize every aspect of her personal choices and personality. Wait — the next couple months?! You mean she kept dating him after that first party? Yes, she did. Remember, I said she was lonely. Loneliness deludes us and makes us forget our dignity, rendering us vulnerable to be abused and to abuse. In the end, the boy didn't want to date this girl; he wanted to date himself. His goal was to make her over into his image. Evil says, "You are not me, but you will be." Goodness says, "You are not me, and I'm glad. In fact, that is why I want and can even have communion with you, because you and I are not the same, nor will we ever be, nor do I want you to be. If you were the same as me, that would be boring." Boredom, as I mentioned previously, is a hallmark of evil. This is true because people who do evil only want to celebrate themselves or one aspect of reality over and over again. "Evil," says Scott Peck, is "a part trying to become a whole."[21] Evil, in other words, is an aspect of reality which "doesn't know its place." It wants to be everything. Even God doesn't want to be everything. God is perfectly content to allow us to continue in communion with Him without trying to co-opt our own unique identities, something that boy on the date would not be happy doing.

Evil takes one thing and makes it everything. As an example, consider the difference between a pornographic novel and a novel with sexual intercourse in it. Pornography takes one part of our sexuality (genitals) and makes it the only thing. It is a form of fetishism. When sex is written about in the context of love and commitment, it retains its proper meaning and causes hardly a ripple of outrage or lust within readers. Evil, on the other hand, disregards context, and spills its private egoistic meanings onto everything. The root of all this disregarding of the other and concentrating upon the self is loneliness.

Another example of what happens to relationships that are dominated by the needs and ego of just one partner came dramatically clear to me after I heard of the following sad story. There was a husband who had the habit of reading pornography and masturbating. These actions continued over many years. Once, when making love to his wife, he realized a terrible thing: in fact, he had not been making love to her or with her. He had not been celebrating their unity in difference, their communion with each other. Rather, he had simply been "masturbating into her," as he said. Here was a glimpse of hell, a pain so deep because of its paradox. At the very moment when one is supposed to be celebrating a mutuality, a communion with spouse, instead he was simply taking what he wanted, and experiencing only the private meaning of lust. For this man, years of self-enclosed pleasure (reading pornography) bore fruit in the inability to transcend the self and encounter another.

The roots of morally evil behavior can be partially pulled up and discarded by opening ourselves to being affected by God and others. Preoccupation with self or refusal to form communities of service and care can only exacerbate our tendency to choose immoral activity. Christ came to enlighten our consciences within a community that worships and adores God. Embedding our lives within the purposes of this community and stemming the ill effects of egoism and loneliness are ways to lessen the appearance of moral evil within our behavior.

If we are really concerned about doing something about evil, we can work hard to create community. Not "touchy-feely" "lifestyle enclaves" where superficial values are affirmed,[22] but honest-to-goodness communities of faith where truth and charity bind one another. We want to be morally good, but we don't have to be all alike in the myriad ways that we speak, act, think, create, play. It is God's desire that we all remain ourselves even as we seek to be *one* in moral goodness. Even the way we express our moral virtue is unique to our personalities and character. The moment we oppress and dictate, we squelch the ability of the Spirit to identify our own gifts, personalities and imaginations and to personally call each of us from within the conscience.

As a result of the power of faith, hope, and love, we can crown our moral lives with the virtue of forgiveness. In this we share most deeply in the paschal mystery of Jesus as we incorporate the wounds inflicted by others into our love for them. When we are ready to forgive, we truly love our enemies. This is the pinnacle of Christian moral disposition.

5

Moral Formation in Daily Life

Many false prophets will arise and deceive many; and because of the increase of evildoing, the love of many will grow cold. But the one who perseveres to the end will be saved" (Mt 24:11-13). Moral evil affects the way we look at the world. It does in fact make our hearts grow cold. Those to whom we have given access to our hearts have the power to form us. What has filled our minds? Whom have we listened to? Note what Matthew says: "Many false prophets will arise." As a result of listening to these "false prophets," our hearts will grow cold. Recently, I read a news story about an increase in theft by workers on the job. Apparently thirty percent of all companies that go out of business each year do so as result of employee theft. Those employees who steal often try to justify their theft by rationalizing that the employer is not paying them enough, or that the employer is rich and can absorb the small losses incurred by their taking what they consider to be trivial items. Surely in this rationalization the heart has grown cold. In this chapter I want to reflect on the importance of some virtues which assist us to live as fully Christian in the context of ordinary life.

The Importance of Sunday

The Ten Commandments, which include the law against stealing, are *not sufficient* unto themselves to promote and motivate moral living, but they are *necessary*. What *is* equally necessary is to find a way not to let our hearts grow cold. The heart, by which I mean our capacity to love others and the moral truth, grows cold by attending to those things that deaden our capacity to transcend the self. It grows cold when we attend to evil, when we listen to the world's materialistic values instead of God's values, and when we fail to promote community. One way to warm the heart is to recover the seventh day of the week as a real day of rest and worship. By doing this we reorient ourselves toward relationships with others and God.

It doesn't surprise me that we have no real day of rest anymore. We have missed the point of rest. Many work right through Sunday, or we shop our Sundays away, or we fill them with activities and events. We fill our restless hearts with products, achievements, and entertainment. Perhaps we do not rest on Sundays because we do not desire what rest is for — relationships.[23] But rest is only fruitful after work, which stems from and aims toward our fulfillment in God. After working hard all week we *get* to rest and we *get* our heart's desire — relationships. We need to be released from the desire to produce and consume, and, instead, celebrate a day filled with people and God. On the day of rest we seek intimacy with others. We tend to *fit* relationships in and *fit* God in on Sunday, when in fact the whole day is intended for re-igniting the heart toward communion with God and others.

Sunday is supposed to burst upon us with a transcendent

flare, reminding us to look up and look ahead and look beyond the end of our nose. As Jacques Ellul once said, "Not everything takes place on earth." The heart grows cold when fare too meager for its expansive nature, such as shopping and entertainment, consume it. Sunday beckons us to enter and enjoy a taste of future glory. Our hearts are certainly restless until they rest in God, as St. Augustine taught. Sunday awaits us, calls to us, inviting us to come rest in God for a while. Do we want to?

It is a virtue to worship God; indeed we are drawn to God through the virtues of faith, hope, and love. But these virtues need to be practiced, and in their exercise they are deepened and then crowned with the gifts of the Holy Spirit (see Is 11:1-2). By the common exercise of these virtues, we are bound to our common object of love. We only gather in parishes because we have responded to a call of love from the one God in Christ and through the Holy Spirit. Being a parish is not like joining a charitable or fraternal organization. Rather, a parish forms by an invitation from God to know God and then lives out that knowledge as a community. This is the core of parish life: responding to this invitation to love God together.

In our devotion to God in the Eucharist and the other sacraments, we come to acquire the pivotal virtue of the love of God. Without this virtue, all our desires can be misdirected and lead us astray. It is worship which helps to center our hearts, enabling us to think clearly about how we ought to act. The love of God fills us and channels our virtues toward the moral good. Living a communal life of loving God in the context of service, study, and worship is the parish life, and it is this life which is the ordinary context for Catholic conscience formation.

Sunday stands as a regular opportunity to purify our concerns and interests. All through the week we are worried and anxious over so many things that we find it difficult to focus upon relationships. We bring our fears to worship, preoccupations that may block our vulnerability to God and continue our egoistic leanings. Worries can be brought to God, of course, but with a disposition of faith. If we cling to things and achievements more than relationships, we will live in fear of losing these things and achievements. Yet we will never lose authentic relationships of love. We may go through periods of absence, as when a friend moves or enters a season that calls for solitude, but even death, the ultimate absence, is not the end of our loves. To put it in economic terms, relationships are a good investment. Fear is lessened when one lives a life around people, not things. This is called the simple life, a life wherein others figure more prominently than the cares and interests of the self, and more than our achievements and goals.

The Simple Life

My family owns a twelve-year-old car that has served us well. My sons, Kristoffer and Jonathan, are rather embarrassed by Dad's "old bomb" of a car. But every morning we climb into it and throw our books on its seats, spill our coffee or orange juice on its floor, and we couldn't care less. We drive to school singing and talking and making stupid and boorish boy jokes. The only thing the old car does well is to give us an excuse to think of one another. In other words, it has been around so long that it has finally become the only thing it was ever supposed to be: a car. It's no longer a status symbol, a badge of success, or a traveling den. It is a car. It takes us places and takes us back again. We feel free in that car because we do not think of the car, we think of one another. The car has no material value — that is what has freed us. But it does have functional value and, without overstating it too much, it also has spiritual value. It is the only place I can remember singing out loud with my sons. That alone is enough to make me cherish the thing, because it allows me to be free to be in communion with Kristoffer and Jonathan. I cherish it, but I do not care about its condition. What I cherish is what it has done for my relationships with my sons.

When the car finally dies I will have some sentimental feelings for the "old bomb." It is associated with my entire married life — it was the first car my wife and I owned after we were married. The sentiment is not about the thing, the car; it is about the memories of living a life with my wife and children. This is why we miss old neighborhoods, homes, or previous jobs. We shouldn't grieve too much for a vacated house or an old employment position, since they are only stages upon which more vital realities occur. But we do rightfully grieve the passing of old friends or colleagues, and we do associate these relationships with things and places. My aunt has a wall full of teacups and saucers — not because she derives some satisfaction from telling people she owns them. Rather, each one is a present from a niece or nephew. It started when she bought herself one nice teacup and placed it on her mantle. After that the family started buying teacups, one after another. Now the cups symbolize the love our family has toward her. It is the family she cherishes in those cups, not the cups. We only value things and give things and places special value as a way of lingering around relationships of love.

There is a dark side to possessing things, however, as I have previously discussed. I may express how detached I am from my old car, and that I couldn't care less whether my boys spill drinks on its floormats or tear its upholstery, but recently I couldn't transfer that kind of freedom from worry to my attitude toward a new kitchen floor we recently purchased. After the new floor was installed I became a veritable tyrant. The minute I heard the side door open I would yell out, "Take your shoes off." I was heard to exclaim quite frequently, "Who walked in here with mud on their shoes?" Each day my family saw me wash the new floor, gazing at its gleam of bright colors. The floor had possessed me because it was new and expensive. Nonetheless, eventually a larger question loomed for me: What did my anger toward my begrimed boys cost me? Would they even want to sing and joke in the old bomb with such a miserable crank for a father? What do I really want, clean floors or singing in the car? I want both! And I achieved both, but not by obsessively coveting my new flooring and seeing each new entrant into the kitchen as the floor's latest enemy. Instead, I achieved an enjoyment of both new floor and old car by coming to see the truth about myself. The condition of my floor and my worry over its cost was obstructing the way of relationships. I was definitely not practicing the virtue of hospitality with my family. Nor was I exhibiting the cheerfulness indicative of one who places one's trust and identity in God. Clearly, I was being a selfish idiot. As is true in all good marriages, Marianne helped me see the extreme absurdity of my position by placing a leftover piece of the new linoleum under the covers of our bed. On it was a note that read, "Dear Jim, I want to give you this quiet intimate moment with the thing you care most about. Love, the other woman." Not only was the note a hilarious jolt back to reality, but also it was painfully accurate. I remembered that it was much more important to focus on my family, not the furnishings.

Since marriage is a sacrament, I know that I encounter Christ within the love my wife and I have for each other. Her note to me was the cold water of truth splashed on my face. The truth is what Christ is all about, and He conspires with wives (and others by the multitudes) to reach out to us and save us from selfishness and stupidity. The more we honor our relationship with Him in our marriage and in our worship life, the more we are able to hear His truth no matter its source. A key to moral conversion and formation is not to be a snob about the vehicles God chooses for instructing us. As we learn in the Scriptures, for instance, something good can come from Nazareth (seeJn 1:46)!

I have come to believe that God loves us so much that our entire day is simply one opportunity after another for Him to draw us closer to himself and move us farther from self-centeredness or self-hate. Christ has re-oriented my poor disposition countless times through a sunrise, the beauty of light upon a certain tree or pond, the raised eyebrow of a co-worker, the laughter of my sons, and the cheerfulness or tears of my wife. There is literally no escape from the overwhelming divine conspiracy to save us from immorality. We, like the mother of Christ, need to embrace an attitude of trusting receptivity. Mary was ready to receive life so deeply that life itself became one with her that she might give birth to Life for us. In our willingness to grow in moral virtue and holiness, we too, in our own way, give birth to life. We become witnesses to the fact that there is more to living than the preoccupations of our little worlds of profession, entertainment, or political ambition. Both the life of morality and worship can be achieved only when we stop taking, stop controlling, and become like Mary: "May it be done to me according to your word" (Lk 1:38). Can we embrace receptivity and let go of our clutching to things, food and technology, for instance, and relinquish a heart which, as I once read somewhere, "clings to my way, the easy way, or no way"? Can we, through God's grace, become liberated from enslavement to ego? Can we learn to cling only to the truth that sets us free? In other words, can we discipline the imagination enough to focus our minds and hearts upon He who liberates us from all that is not real? Yes, of course we can — it is called being Catholic. It is the simple life.

God's Mercy

In being Catholic we are open to receive both wisdom and mercy from God in Christ as we discern what is right and wrong. When we sin and fail to live in reality, do we seek and then accept the mercy of God? God's mercy is a "special kind of love which prevails over sin."[24] The mercy of God is what mends and heals and reconciles the sinner to Love itself. Mercy is a divine power that brings sinners back into relatedness with God and one another. To cry out for this mercy is a grace given to us by our baptismal identities (see 1 Pt 1:3). This mercy is bestowed when one's heart, or a community's conscience, recognizes its sin, names it, and cries out to Christ like Bartimaeus did, "Son of David, have pity on me." As I mentioned in my reference to the Morris scandal, naming the sin is crucial for living in the truth. Our minds are so adept at self-deception that simply making a general prayer of repentance leaves many corners within our hearts still in darkness. We need, for our sake, to name our sins and own them and in grace struggle to overcome them by the mercy of God. "If we say, 'We are without sin,' we deceive ourselves, and the truth is not in us. If we acknowledge our sins, he is faithful and just and will forgive our sins and cleanse us from every wrongdoing" (1 Jn 1:8-9).

Recently I had a particularly grace-filled celebration of the Sacrament of Reconciliation. After the priest finished reciting the Prayer of Absolution, I got up to leave the reconciliation room and he stopped me, saying, "When you leave here, it is as if you have been born again; trust in the mercy of God." The moral life draws its power from the mercy of God; God wants us to be good. He is, in a sense, rooting for us to become saints. The Church realized this truth and composed a tremendous prayer of absolution that highlights that God's merciful love is for our conversion.

> God, the Father of mercies,
> through the death and resurrection of his Son
> has reconciled the world to himself
> and sent the Holy Spirit among us
> for the forgiveness of sins;
> through the ministry of the Church
> may God give you pardon and peace,
> and I absolve you from your sins
> in the name of the Father, and of the Son,
> and of the Holy Spirit.
>
> — from the *Rite of Penance*

The Mind of Christ

We are called upon to name our sins and entrust ourselves to the mercy of God, and then we will receive the wisdom to know His will regarding moral behavior. As Paul writes:

> I appeal to you therefore, brothers and sisters, by the mercies of God, to present your bodies as a living sacrifice, holy and acceptable to God, which is your spiritual worship. Do not be conformed to this world, but be transformed by the renewing of your mind, so that you may discern what is the will of God — what is good and acceptable and perfect (Rm 12:1-2, NRSV).

Worship leads to insight about one's moral state before God. By the power of the word of God, prayer, and sacrament, we are ushered into knowledge about God and about our own state before God. Paul urges us to offer *ourselves*, not things, to God in worship. Our self-offering enables us to join in the self-offering of Christ upon the cross. We then become one with Christ and are invited to live a life like Him.

Living a life as Christ did means living a life that is centered upon listening to the Father.

> The way we may be sure that we know him is to keep his commandments. Whoever says, 'I know him,' but does not keep his commandments is a liar, and the truth is not in him. But whoever keeps his word, the love of God is truly perfected in him. This is the way we may know that we are in union with him: whoever claims to abide in him ought to live just as he lived (1 Jn 2:3-6).

The mind is transformed in listening to the Father through Christ. We take on the mind of Christ and begin to think as one who is beloved by the Father. Because of this we can ask what is usually perceived to be a childish question: What would Jesus do in this situation? To answer this question, one does not have to become a Biblical fundamentalist. In fact, literal interpretation of the Bible is not always appropriate in ethical discernment. Some behaviors indicated in Scripture seem to be metaphorical (e.g. "turn the other cheek"; see Mt 5:39), while others, such as the command against murder, are more literal. Further, if we interpret the Scriptures literally, we are forced to conclude that there is no Christian answer to many contemporary medical, sexual, and social questions, as these do not appear in Scripture (for example, in vitro fertilization). To have the mind of Christ does not mean we simply mouth Scriptural answers. To have the mind of Christ means to be conformed to Christ through *a loving devotion* to Him in worship, study, and service to the community. Being thus formed, our minds are "renewed" (see Rom 12:2) and we have taken on the "mind of Christ" (1 Cor 2:16). The Christian judges right and wrong behavior as one who possesses the mind of Christ, not simply with his or her own mind. The Christian mind has been filled with the Spirit of God. Recall Jeremiah 31:33, where the prophet says that God will place His law within us and write it upon our hearts. We have the mind of Christ because we have been given the Spirit of God, the Spirit that cries out "Abba, Father!" (Gal 4:6).

The moral decisions we make as Catholics must have their source deep within our identity — our oneness with Christ. We are, like Christ, persons who listen to the Father. Listening is not some mindless obedience. It is a chance to re-orient our minds away from personal opinions, political slogans, and habitual reactions, and think like one who has been transformed by lovingly attending to the truths of faith within the Church. The Scriptures report that in order to be sure He was acting out of the dignity of His identity as "beloved son" (Mt 17:5), Christ did not act until He prayed, until He listened to the Father.

Obedience

As Jesus listened to the Father, so we are to listen to Christ. This listening is not a form of childish obedience wherein a parent would yell in exasperation, "Do this because I told you to!" The listening needed for sound moral decision-making is the kind of listening that is present in an encounter between two adults, between two centers of freedom, between two persons of dignity. Obedience is an ugly word today because we imagine obedient ones cowering under a dictator who wields abusive authority, or we envision a pathological pastor who approaches his people out of fear and consequently pastors them into fear. Certainly the abuses of authority are tragic and real. But we must recover a positive, Christ-like understanding of the virtue of obedience if we are ever to have our minds formed by the Spirit of God. In Christ we have a new kind of obedience. It is not constricting or oppressive. Rather, as Christian, to be obedient is simply to be faithful to who we are at our deepest center: related to Christ in love. To know Christ's love is to be schooled in an obedience that arises not from some outside source or authority but from the very Spirit itself. The Spirit engenders within us an eagerness to raptly listen to and for the truths of Christ no matter in what forum they may appear. The eagerness to listen to Christ is a positive desire to simply listen to the one we love. Do we love Christ? This becomes the crucial question.

The obedience needed in Christian ethics is more akin to the attention two lovers give to one another than to the response given to a judge or police officer. The two lovers cannot hear enough from and about the other. It is not unusual for those who are in love to stay up half the night talking with each other and listening intently to the beloved. To the demands of police officers and judges, however, we simply comply. This legal model is not the model needed for Christian ethics. Eventually, when the two lovers get married, their love takes on a public meaning; so it is for those who love Christ. We cannot simply listen to Christ in the secret place of our conscience; we must allow the fruit of that conversation to blossom in public. All hidden conversation with Christ about ethics becomes public in *our character* and in *our action.* There is nothing private about an ethic based on love of God. Just as the love between spouses becomes the foundation for the *public good* of the family they become, so our obedience to Christ is for the good of the world and for our own good. To be obedient to Christ's teaching within the Church *is* simply our way of loving Him (see Jn 14:15).

Purifying Our Desires

As a Catholic obeys Christ within the conscience, he or she goes deeper and deeper into the shared life of the paschal mystery — Christ's life, death, and resurrection. We are, in other words, living out our baptism. The baptized life becomes our way of being in the world. To enable obedience, the Spirit arouses our desire to listen in love and simultaneously purifies any desires to sin. This purification is necessary because we are not yet fully one with Christ in our listening to moral truth. The Spirit purifies our desire to simply choose what we want, and instructs us to instead desire what is morally good.

We experience the pain of resisting conversion from sin when we rationalize or excuse our behavior. Through this excusing and rationalizing, we are simply avoiding the inevitable: painfully confronting the truth of our moral condition before God. For example, I remember when I was a small boy I broke a jar filled with cookies in our kitchen. My mother asked if I had broken the jar, but I said "No." Since my mother knew I was the only one home and therefore must have broken the cookie jar, she gently probed a little more and gave me the opportunity to name my own act and not lie. "Are you sure you didn't break it?" she asked. I looked at my shoes. She came closer and, putting her hand under my chin, directed me to look at her when she was speaking. I slowly looked up, but still could not look into her eyes. She told me to do so. I did and I started to cry. "Yes," I said, "I broke it." She hugged me and told me always to tell the truth.

I have come to see this childhood incident as a metaphor for purgatory and the purification that is necessary in order to be in full communion with Love and Truth itself. Someday we all must "face God" and live (see Ex 33:20). That life is called heaven. But first we must face God and die — we must die to sin. The doctrine of purgatory simply acknowledges that when we die we will look at truth itself, and it will be painful because we are not fully aligned with those realities. We will want to look at the floor, but God, the Father of Mercies, will ask us to look at Him when He's speaking. In that moment when we look at God, we will be simultaneously cleansed of sin and united with Him. Our purgatory can begin here if we begin to look at truth now. Christian morality is not about freedom of choice; it is only about the freedom to be good. The parish exists, in its sacraments and service, to help us look at whether we are becoming good and whether we are giving obedience to the ultimate authority, God. The less we form our consciences by listening to "this age" (Rom 12:2), the less we will have to be purified in the face of real Love and Truth.

To educate our consciences, we are called through baptism to deeply enter the practices, rituals, and customs of the Catholic parish. Americans *think* we want to be objective and neutral regarding ethics. We *think* we want empty categories of moral analysis so we can all decide for ourselves what is right and wrong and, therefore, all feel good about ourselves for deciding, for choosing. But in reality we know that there is no neutral moral ground. Are we with Christ or against Him? We are either formed in the sensibilities of Catholicism, or we are formed in the sensibilities of some other authority? This is where choice comes in: "Decide today whom you will serve. . . .

As for me and my household, we will serve the LORD" (Jos 24:15).

We live in a parish community because it is that community which facilitates our growth in virtue. We cannot be virtuous without one another. We need models and examples. Yes, the parish will hurt us as well. People within it will be petty and selfish and break faith, but what is the alternative? Do we want to stay away from the parish altogether, or do we want to go parish-hopping? Or, worse, do we want to break away from the Catholic Church and start yet another Christian denomination? That is one thing the world does not need, another Christian community claiming to be "more Christian" than the hundreds already in existence. *All* Christian denominations have two things in common: They are filled with sinners and they all cry out for mercy to the Savior. Since the parish is filled with both sinners and saints, we will be able to emulate the saints among us by practicing one of their prime virtues toward sinners, forgiveness. And the more we keep emulating the saints and forgiving the sinners, the more we will become saints and add to the ranks of the holy among us. Then our parishes will truly be yeast for the secular world. This yeast is the moral truth known by our abiding in and with Christ.

The moral life is one focused upon relationships of dignity between God and us. We are forced in a contemporary, consumerist society to conform to images of self that mute relationships of love and justice, and exalt achievement and the material. The moral life is more about receiving than achieving. It is more about being than having. If we are *faithful* to our deepest identity in God, we will have found our most reliable source of moral wisdom. God shared this deepest identity with us in Jesus Christ — to be simply good and purified of all that is beneath our dignity, listen to Him in the midst of the Church and "do whatever he tells you" (Jn 2:5).

6

Moral Discernment in the Local Community of Saints

A Moral Miracle

E ven the best of parishes need to look beyond their own members to the lives of those who have gone before us, especially the canonized saints. Knowing the saints and calling upon them for prayer and guidance further establishes our knowledge that the power needed to become good and to trust God is not contained simply on earth. Knowing the virtues and behaviors of the saints stimulates our own moral imaginations. The saints teach us that in living lives of deep trust in God, becoming good is *more* than possible for each of us. One saint that my family has particular devotion to interceded for Marianne and me before God for a "moral miracle."

A moral miracle is an act of grace that transforms our attitudes and dispositions toward what is good and holy. Our moral miracle happened soon after the birth of our second son, Jonathan. At that time Marianne was experiencing mild fatigue and an inability to coordinate a few simple movements such as lifting her arm and walking in a confident manner. We went to the doctor for another problem and off-handedly commented upon these symptoms. He immediately set up an appointment with a neurologist. In the end, we discovered that Marianne has multiple sclerosis (MS). We were devastated and heartbroken. Marianne was afraid. I assumed she was afraid of what I was afraid of: her impending paralysis and the very real possibility of life in a wheelchair. I came to find out that her fear was not centered upon those physical limitations, per se, but upon what those limitations would do to her ability to be a good mother to our sons. Losing the ability to care for our children was her greatest fear.

We began to pray for Marianne's healing to one of our favorite family saints, Venerable Father Solanus Casey, O.F.M. Cap. My grandmother knew Father Solanus when he served Sacred Heart Church in Yonkers, New York. People had come to regard Solanus as a holy man because he had the power to heal those whom illness afflicted. Even though he died in 1957, I grew up with the Capuchin Franciscan as practically a family friend, because his memory was so present in our family. Both Marianne and I turned to Solanus with prayers for healing, but we aimed at different maladies. I prayed that she would be rid of MS; she prayed that despite her MS she could still be a good mother. The miracle happened soon after Marianne's hospitalization for treatments with the drug ACTH. As she was lying in the hospital bed, two Franciscan friars came into her room and began to converse with her. They had heard that she was in the hospital through their work in our parish. When Marianne told them about her MS, one of the friars smiled broadly and said, "Oh, my mother has MS, and she is the greatest mother of all time!" He went on to tell wonderful stories of his mother and how she excelled in all the virtues needed to raise children in faith. Marianne was struck to the deepest part of her heart and felt the burdens of sadness and fear lift from her. Father Solanus had sent one of his brothers to comfort Marianne and affirm that she too could excel in virtue as a mother, despite her terrible disease. The friars prayed with her and for her and then left the hospital room.

Many years have passed since the diagnosis, and Marianne is still being another "greatest mother of all time." The saints want to empower us to be good through their prayers, to excel at our vocations, and to achieve a high level of virtue just as they did. To neglect to pray with them for our own moral development is a tragic spiritual oversight. Marianne has not been cured of her disease, but she was cured of the *fear* that could have crippled her ability to go on being loving, hospitable, disciplined, and joyful. She was healed of an obstruction to holiness. Her disease by itself does not block holiness, which is the only goal we *need* to attain. But the attitude with which we approach our diseases or circumstances can indeed either facilitate or negate our cooperation with the grace God wants to give us in our individual vocations as married, single, or religious.

The canonized saints not only give us examples through their lives, but also, now that they reside with God in heaven, they unleash the power we have within us to love what is good. Marianne knew what was good — the welfare of our children — and in asking for what was good, "it [was] not [to] be taken from her" (Lk 10:42). The fruit of desiring to be morally good is not usually seen in worldly success, but it is always seen in the birth of a person's new character. In the grace of God's moral miracle through the prayers of Venerable Solanus Casey, Marianne lives with MS with new courage, faith, hope, and love for God and family.

Why do we continue to neglect the saints and their prayers

for our own moral conversions? Many shy away from devotion to saints because they fear that it looks as if they are replacing due worship of Christ with such saintly devotion. Nothing could be further from the truth. We do not pray *to* saints — we ask them to pray *for* and *with* us. If we believe that life goes on in Christ for all eternity, then the saints are living still in God and continue to worship and adore and love God. Just as we would ask a fellow Christian on earth to pray for our needs, we ask our fellow Christians in heaven to do the same.

The Parish and Moral Discernment

The moral life is both a gift and a struggle. To become good, one needs models of virtue and friends who share common beliefs. The saints serve that purpose, as do our fellow parishioners and family members. We all need to look to the lives of those who live the faith. Of course there is moral failure all around us. But it is not helpful to become too downcast about the sinfulness of church leaders and members. Fixation upon others' failures only leads to sarcasm, cynicism, and gossip. I am not saying that we should dismiss the moral failures of others as inconsequential, because, in fact, the most urgent call today for those serving as leaders in the parish — be they priests or laypeople — is the call to repentance. The formation, and where needed the re-formation, of true spiritual leaders is what parishes most need today. Leaders who desire holiness themselves will instill the desire for holiness in parishioners. Holiness is not a pre-requisite for pastoral leadership, but the desire for it is. The important thing to remember is that just as moral failure surrounds us, so do moral courage and virtue. We need to look to the latter.

In these days, when even Catholics have rejected so much of the Church's objective moral teaching, just living the Ten Commandments can be seen as an act of heroic virtue. Recall the women's reactions to the television announcement that Dick Morris' wife would forgive him. The virtue of forgiveness is a standard Christian disposition, hardly controversial, and yet it was belittled when exhibited by Morris's wife. Since so much of American culture rejects the moral counsel of the Church in the areas of marriage and divorce, sexuality, artificial repro-duction, assisted suicide, workplace justice, abortion, and capi-tal punishment, among others, many find it very difficult to actually live according to Catholic moral principles.

The parish is to be the place where the moral teachings of Christ are taught, appropriated, and practiced. The parish should be the place where these teachings are cherished, and where inquiry into their truth is fostered. No doubt people will dis-agree with the teachings of the Church on moral issues. This has always been and always will be true. The danger today is the presence of widespread, unreflected *bias against* the moral teachings of the Church. It is difficult in some parishes to even give these teachings a fair hearing. Nevertheless, those who disagree with the moral teachings of the Church are not to be shunned or rejected in any manner. They are our brothers and sisters in Christ. Only the power of persuasion is to be brought against them. We are to trust in God and in the force of our faith-imbued reason.[25]

Furthermore, the parish is not a graduate school or secular university. It does not try to be an empty container where our various opinions and theories are given the same weight as the doctrine and witness of Jesus Christ. The parish — as it is symbolized in its leadership and ministries of the word, sacra-ment, and service — *knows what it is about* even if some mem-bers wish to promote a change in doctrine through their per-sonal acts of dissent. History *has* shown that there has been some change over time in the moral teachings and practices of the Church. This is indisputable. We were a Church that once sanctioned the torture of heretics, forced religious conversions, and tolerated the ownership of slaves. And so it would seem, in light of past experience, that we must remain open to the possibility that our minds might one day see moral evil where once we saw goodness, or where we saw right judgment now see error. Can we have parishes that *cherish the tradition*, while *disinguishing irreformable teaching from current ecclesiastical discipline*, all within a community that reveres conscience formation and its exercise? Yes, I believe we can. Cultivating this kind of communal disposition should be a pastoral priority.

Even though we acknowledge a development in moral doctrine, we do not have to conclude that all moral teaching is constantly in flux. The list of moral truths and doctrines that have remained stable for thousands of years is itself a testament to the promise of God to teach us the truth. And, the development of moral doctrine is a witness to the fact that God still abides with us, *teaching* and *correcting* where needed. What the parish needs to do is to equip its members with the skills of moral discernment. Catholics *want* to be open to the truth, as the Church perceives it. Even still, we also have the right to exercise our own minds and freedom in the process of being taught. Without such freedom, any reception of Church moral teaching by its adult members simply becomes an act of blind obedience, a kind of obedience that is without merit. In authentic obedience, one needs to appropriate the truth of moral doctrine *for oneself.*[26] For an act to be "yours," it needs to be understood and freely undertaken or adhered to. This freedom is to be exercised in a process of moral decision-making, the components of which I will outline now.

1. One of the most vital components of moral decision-making is the interior attitude possessed by the one making the decision. We need to approach the teachings of the Church with a teachable mind. It is never a requirement, however, for one to accept everything that the Church teaches as *infallibly* true; even the bishops don't do that. But the question of attitude is crucial because it embodies how one approaches the entire task of moral discernment. If, for example, one begrudges the need for a teacher or begins the inquiry with a bias *against*

Scripture or the bishops, then real moral decisions will be born only if that person is first re-directed to explore that personal bias. Only after the bias and its origin have been identified may the person then go on to explore the moral question at hand. Any pre-existing bias against Church sources or authority does not have to be healed completely before investigating the moral question, per se, as healing often occurs through the discernment process itself. In the case of bias against the Church, I would recommend that persons sit down with a lay minister or cleric and simply *listen* to the Church's position; the minister should then simply *listen* to the inquirer's position. Often the inquirer's bias was not held in contempt but in ignorance, and listening to one another enables persons to begin to form the conscience again in light of an ecclesial identity. This kind of consultation attempts to clarify the facts of one's contemplated behavior. What am I really doing when I do this act? Who am I becoming through this kind of behavior?

2. The next component in moral decision-making is to immerse oneself in prayer. Prayer is an expression of our minds and hearts communing with God. Our relationship with God figures prominently into the process of looking for the moral truth, because God enlightens us by identifying the moral truth. We want to be open to God in our depths so that we can listen to the truth. And, since living morally defines who I am, I want to involve God in this deepest part of my identity — my response to the judgments of conscience. Moreover, since our identity is totally wrapped up in God, it would be nonsensical to bracket out our relationship with God during the discernment process. To do so would be like a married person who makes all family decisions by him- or herself, eschewing the very relationship with spouse that makes up the core of the marital identity. To say the least, a spouse who did such an act would not be living in reality. So it is with moral decision-making. If we claim Catholicism as our community of salva-

tion, to disregard the very core of that identity during moral decision-making — being in God — is to deny reality. By soaking the moral decision-making process in prayer, I acknowledge that this decision is about who I am becoming in my relationships with God and others. I want God in on it! People who pray joyfully receive the truth about their moral state and seek insight and repentance where necessary. To pray our way through moral discernment is simply a way of affirming our radical identity in God.

3. Next, we should consult with other Christians and Christian sources about the decision. I recall an incident when a neighbor came to my house to visit. Soon the conversation turned to his personal life as he announced his impending divorce. He wanted to know what I thought of that. I asked whom he had consulted about his decision, and he mentioned his wife first. That was a good start, I thought. Then he went on to list several consultants: "I spoke to Bruce down the street who is divorced; I read a little in a book about divorce; and I had a conversation with my parents." These are not bad sources of conscience formation, but they seem inadequate for someone who lives the baptized life as a Catholic, as this man did. Why didn't he pray, go for marriage counseling, talk to a priest, go on retreat, take his wife away on vacation, and/or separate for a while and work hard on changing the obstacles of intimacy? For one who attends Mass every Sunday, as I knew he did, I found it odd that he didn't see his chosen sources as rather anemic. Whether or not his divorce could be justified or tolerated morally is a question I cannot answer here. But I am morally certain that he did not make his decision out of an explicit consciousness of his baptismal identity, which is the only identity that matters in eternity. Each of these components for discernment — disposition, prayer, and consultation — should not be artificially segmented as steps in a recipe, but apportioned throughout a dedicated life of faith.

Pastoral Compassion

I once spoke with someone who was seriously entertaining the option of assisted suicide as his cancer progressed. He did not want to become a burden to his family, thus his act of suicide would be partially motivated out of his love for his family. The path he was thinking about choosing to *express* this love, however, was not a worthy vehicle for such a beautiful motive. In morality, both the *intention* and the *object* of the act must be sufficiently worthy or the act cannot be done. To show love for others by killing oneself contradicts the loving intent of the act and should be rejected. It is important to note that this man was a good man — he was aware of his family's pain and wanted to ease their suffering while he was dying. It would have been an insult to him and his love for his family to simply make a pronouncement *against* his desire for suicide. Certainly killing oneself is an objectively evil act, but we must see the person within a broader context. The pastoral task is to acknowledge the good that is present, as well as the temptations toward evil, all the while speaking a word of hope.

Moral evil would be easy to condemn outright if it didn't constantly raise its head within the wills and minds of such beautiful and good persons as the patient just described. How easy it would be to yell out, "You fornicators and adulterers are going to hell!" But all of a sudden you glimpse a divorced Catholic who has remarried outside the Church whom you know and love. Or you see a college student whom you know to be having sex outside of marriage, but who also embodies care and sensitivity toward children and the poor like few you have known. Yes, adultery is wrong, as is fornication, as is killing oneself, but in the varied contexts of real life it takes more love, prudence, wisdom, and courage to call people away from these acts than one might at first sense. This is true because we are all caught in the web of sin. We empathize with those in sin, and we remember our own weaknesses and struggles against sin, past or present, and we take a deep breath and yield over to God in prayer the true needs of our fellow believers.

And yet the Church is summoned by truth to preach what is right in and out of season. In anger and frustration we may want to throw the book at our fellow Catholics or we may, alternately, want to tell them the book is irrelevant. Rather than serving the moral needs of parishioners, both extremes simply serve our needs to either quickly get through ambiguity or avoid rejection. This entanglement of all of us in sin and grace is experienced deeply in parish life. There the weeds and wheat grow together and will do so until the end of time. We are called to live among the weeds and wheat and to tug gingerly at the weeds so that the wheat may get more light, air, and fertile soil. Each grain of wheat is precious, and to yank out the weeds may harm the wheat and the goodness already within (see Mt 13:24-30). And so we gently yet persistently abide with one another. We endure the sins of one another, forgiving one another, and celebrating the grace within one another, as we give thanks and lift up to God in adoration and worship our whole communal life.

We need to consult our pastoral minister for assistance in moral discernment — he or she can often patiently help us identify objective moral evil. Patience is vital to moral discernment. Without patience the minister might rush consultations along and do violence to the conversion process. We need to be especially patient in our families as well. As a father I have grown angry with my sons. The anger arose from their mistake, but many times my anger was grounded in my own selfishness. Let's say that Kristoffer and Jonathan left some of their toys on the front lawn. I have told them again and again that their laziness is wrong, and that they need to put their things away when they're finished using them. I find my sons and start yelling; they recoil with heads down and do the cleanup in fear and hate. Why did I yell? The anger arose because my authority was spurned; I felt they didn't respect me. The anger arose because I had a problem with my ego being bruised. In actuality, the real problem wasn't my bruised ego at all but simply the toys on the lawn. Why did I turn their forgetfulness into a personal rejection of my parental authority? The answer resides in our sinful leanings. On the days when I am not so egocentric, I notice that I can still correct my boys, but without the huffing and puffing that betray a damaged ego at work. I can abide with them in their growing pains, instruct them, and even maintain relationship with them after the correction is through. Displaced anger is *for* the one who is angry. It usually doesn't serve those who are in error. Rooted in fear and self-centeredness, anger serves the angry one by speeding up time. The angry one has no time to abide with those who have yet to make responsibility, chastity, or prudence a virtue. Of course immoral decisions are costly to community, human character, and individual destiny, but the God whom we serve chooses to abide with us and suffer with us — not make us suffer — as he unfolds truth before us. To be patient means to be able to suffer. Can we suffer the sins of others, cry for them and with them as God's grace works miracles through those prayers, tears, instruction, and our own abiding presence?

The Certainty of Catholic Moral Teaching

How should we think about the *assured* nature of Catholic moral instruction? We have learned over the last twenty-five years that the conscience starves and goes wandering far from the food of Scripture, sacrament, and doctrine if it is not intentionally instructed within those realities. To form conscience without the necessary doctrinal and narrative content from Scripture and saints' lives is to leave students and parishioners directionless. The fallout from a "do what you will as long as you follow your conscience" philosophy is readily seen in the greed of consumeristic lifestyles, the high divorce rate, significant levels of sexually transmitted diseases or teen pregnancies, not to mention contraception and abortions. Are we really freer because one out of two marriages ends in divorce, or because many people will never know the gift of being a virgin on their wedding night, dragging instead the ghosts of many past lovers into their marriage? Are we really free simply because we can choose to buy anything we want and so conspire to reduce our own identities to mere economics? Are we really free because we have no explicit ecclesial teachers but a whole raft of implicit cultural teachers within media, politics, and education that we cannot name?

Trusting in the certainty of ecclesial teaching is not a vice. It is in fact the virtue of humility enacted. It is a stance which says, "I do not always know what to choose," "I do not always know what is morally good," and "I need to look to something beyond myself to contemplate moral truth." Affirming the certainty of Catholic moral teaching can be approached in a calm yet eager manner. We are eager because we know that the very dignity of humanity is at stake when these teachings are rejected. The teaching is also to be transmitted calmly yet firmly, so that it can be allowed to work its way into our hearts. Believers, teachers, and preachers need not equivocate or be paralyzed in their presentations; the truth will win its own victories. The parish needs to continually work to build a community where the truth is longed for, recognized, and cherished. If this is not accomplished, we may be unable to identify the truth when it does instantiate itself in preaching, holiness, or teaching. Moral conversion begins after the truth is named, so the pastoral minister needs to communicate to parishioners a confidence in the moral doctrine of the Church.

Recently I heard a story of a minister in a poor urban church who held worship services that lasted for over three hours on Sunday mornings. When asked why he kept his people in prayer and worship for so long, he answered, "These people are poor; they think they are nothing. The entire economic culture reminds them of that all week. It takes me three hours to get their heads screwed on straight again; they are poor, yes, but they are also the beloved of God." Similarly, I wonder if wealthy parishes need a three-hour service for parishioners to "get their heads screwed on straight." All week wealthy people are told that they are "everything," that they are very important people who are crucial to the success of the economy. Perhaps they, too, need three-hour worship services so they can be exorcised of the myths the culture tells *them* about themselves. This culture tells rich *and* poor that they are either everything or nothing according to what they own or lack. God's reality, however, is that we are all *dignified* — but not because of what we own or don't own. God's children, materially rich *or* poor, are wealthy because of who we *are*: beloved of God. Perhaps we all need three-hour weekly worship services in order to be reminded of this one example of how the world can misdirect our thinking!

In order to recognize the certainty of Catholic moral teaching, one has to be immersed in worship and hold secular cultural values at a critical distance. This is not to say that secular is synonymous with moral evil; in fact, God can teach the Church much through the secular, and He often does. What it does mean is that we will trust our teaching more if we actually live the Catholic life. Like those people who stay in worship for three hours, the more we are aware of our dignity, the more we will understand and practice the moral truths taught by the Church. It is the love of God which "screws our heads on straight."

Social Ethics

A parish community is not only to develop a personal conscience within its parishioners, but is also charged to assist us in developing a *social* conscience. A social conscience is the ability we have to think about what is good and bad for society *as a whole*, in its institutions, patterns of law, and customs. The goal of developing a social conscience is to help people become more aware of how their individual choices become institutionally concretized in the habits, customs, and "ways of doing things" of a society. Over time our personal choices become institutional "structures," our ways of organizing and operating the social institutions of government, business, education, and church. This structure takes on a life of its own and becomes the "way we have always done things." A certain amount of activity and structure should become second nature — this makes an institution's daily routine more effective. Occasionally, however, we should reflect upon the way things are being done in order to see if any one person or group is being left out or barred from participating in the institution. Is there any injustice in our reliance on a certain structure and routine? Structure can give us a framework for acting toward a goal and can even facilitate that goal, but if it is not reassessed occasionally, it might become an end in itself. Instead of serving the needs of people, institutions that go unexamined may become self-serving.

A parish with a social conscience will want to strive to become a model of justice for other institutions. The Catholic conscience doesn't simply look to private or personal behavior and seek its conversion, but seeks to judge the behavior of the community and call the people to conversion where needed. In doing so, the parish becomes a forum for faith formation in those who structure government, business, and education in American culture. Our American culture makes claims on us without our awareness. American values such as individuality, privacy, consumption, youth, and health are in the very air we breathe. By themselves none of these values is evil. They are simply incomplete. Positively, we are also a culture that is very charitable. The charity, however, is overwhelmingly monetary. We have a harder time giving of *ourselves* to those in need. Being American is wonderful, but it is only part of our identity — being Christian is the fullness of our identity. Since we develop into adults with thought patterns that are influenced by American popular, political, and economic culture, it is impossible *not* to be so affected. All along, however, our baptismal identity should be forming *Christian* thought patterns. These thought patterns originate in the very stuff of parish formation: liturgy, religious education, and service. The quality and depth of our Christian conscience depends upon how seriously we attend to our baptismal identity. In the next chapter I will look upon the content of this identity. What is it about the faith experience that makes our conscience specifically *Christian*?

7

Our Religious Identity as a Source of Moral Goodness

hrist's death on the cross holds a most profound place in the consciousness of those baptized into His church. The crucifixion is not simply a historical event, but a present activity that Christians claim a share in every time they worship at the Eucharist and every time they stand for the truth as appropriated by their consciences. In this chapter I will discuss the meaning of moral living in the context of the major Christian mysteries: crucifixion, resurrection, Eucharist, and love. It is out of these mysteries that the Christian draws the power and ability to be good and choose rightly. This ability is given to us because in living out of these mysteries we share in the life of Christ.

Crucifixion

All Christians share in the cross when they choose morally right behavior in spite of painful or mortal consequences. Christians are especially close to the crucified Christ when they suffer the negative social consequences of doing what is morally right. The believer witnesses to the enabling power of the Holy Spirit when choosing the right behavior in the face of others' derision or criticism. Doing what is morally right in the face of negative or evil consequences is not simply the result of our willing it. We can only come to the point of faithfully choosing the right, despite painful consequences, through virtue and grace.

To meet evil with goodness and love is to be "crucified," and sometimes the conscience calls believers to undergo this kind of pain. We know this crucifixion when we are faithful to non-violence in the face of anger, or when we remain faithful to the truth despite its personal costs. We never take up the cross ourselves, however; God offers it to us as a way to embrace the truth. In fact, I would be wary of someone who too quickly invoked the sacred symbol of the cross and used it to represent the spiritual meaning of the ordinary burdens of daily life. The cross is a special experience of confronting evil with love; it is not to be trivialized by aligning it with one's household chores or daily commitments to work or relationships. These activities certainly are graced and can be toilsome, but they normally do not engage us at the depths of our conscience where divine proddings to do the good meet evil inclinations to resist the good. To overcome those inclinations in Christ is to share in the sufferings of Christ's cross.

Sharing in the passion of Christ means not giving in to the hopelessness of vice in the face of the suffering that moral goodness may ask of us. In following our conscience, we share in Christ's will for us to cling to the truth, as He did when He heard it from the Father, mediated by the Spirit within Him. Christ embraces truth even though it kills Him. This is why we

Christians have venerated generation after generation of martyrs: They would rather die than betray the truth of which their conscience convinces them.[27]

But note how brave one has to be in order to do the right thing when everyone else is saying "compromise" and "shirk the call of moral truth." We can do nothing that is truly ours without virtue, and in this case the virtue needed is courage. We cannot develop virtue without having it formed within us through practice. But we must have a community within which to practice virtue and have our virtues affirmed. Where will courage come from if one has not seen it modeled in the parish or the family, or tested it through choices that were later affirmed by the community? The cross will certainly look like the throne of fools if we do not describe, enact, and affirm the courage that is needed to be good. Recall again the response to Mrs. Morris, who said she would forgive her husband's adultery: utter contempt for such stupidity. How will moral goodness flourish if the community disdains it when enfleshed in people's real life decisions?

At a recent parish picnic I attended, a group of friends and I were eating and talking when a disturbance arose on the open field where the children were playing. In the middle of the fray was a woman parishioner — some children were tying soda pop cans to helium-filled balloons, and she was taking them away. She was telling them about the environmental hazards of littering the landscape with cans and balloons. My friends and I laughed and thought her actions were extreme. She even came over to us to express her frustration at the children's actions. After she left we mocked her gently. A few seconds later, however, I became uncomfortable because actually I agreed with her that the landscape should not be filled with such litter, but I had showed no courage in supporting her in her "exaggerated" cause. If I cannot show courage in small causes, when will I practice it in order to be prepared to defend major causes?

Resurrection

Not only should the Lord's cross be within our minds as we come to regard the moral decisions before us, but so also should the fruit of His difficult and faithful act, the resurrection. Our hope is grounded in the Father's act of raising Christ to new life in Him. We can claim this as our hope because Christ has claimed us for Himself through our baptism. We indeed share in the life, death, and resurrection of Christ, because, as Paul said, "yet I live, no longer I, but Christ lives in me" (Gal 2:20). The resurrection will be for us the gift of eternal life, but it begins here in the hope and trust that inhabits our mind and heart and direct our acts of conscience. Through the cross and beyond, and in light of the resurrection, we know that our lives have meaning. Being formed in resurrection thinking helps us in those moments when all we have to cling to is God's promise to be faithful to us. The baptized life is a life of trusting in God's promises and making promises to one another out of the power of the God Who stood by us all. Since we are sinners, we will on occasion have to seek reconciliation and forgiveness for the times we have been unfaithful to the virtuous life. But we do not lose hope. This hope is the crucial mark of the baptized one who seeks a life of virtue. Hope steadies us in times of trial and distress. Hope is a fruit of the resurrection, and this hope pervades our crucifixion moments.

Hope is also instilled through the parish community wherein we keep the stories of resurrection before us and seek to enflesh them in our own lives. Each time we meet moral evil with the truth, without losing hope, and are transformed by this fidelity, we see a glimpse of our new life in God. I recall a family I knew who showed the hope of the resurrected life during a particularly difficult time: the birth of their grandchild to their single teenage daughter. Devastated by the announcement that their daughter was pregnant, they nonetheless focused upon the good that was present amidst those challenging circumstances. They never lost sight of the fact that they were a family and that soon another precious member was to be welcomed into their home. The pregnancy of their single daughter and the impending birth of her child were both emotionally and financially burdensome. There is nothing romantic or sentimental about such a situation; all situations like this are immersed in pain. There is, however, something morally good: the hospitality shown to this new baby by the grandparents, in whose home the baby was to live as the daughter finished high school and college. After the birth, I saw the love of that family, which included the new baby's father, grow to include the new child as they all came to believe they never could have been a family without her! Something that was not asked for, not even dreamed of — a new baby — was given and incorporated into their lives of faith. The baby and the impending wedding of the daughter to the baby's father have now been transformed into a blessing. The resurrected life gives us eyes to see hope where there is none. Life's circumstances challenge us to trust in God alone and His promises of love and goodness. In faith, we can see what may be an objectively difficult situation (for example, pregnancy outside of marriage) through to transformation and a touch of glory. None of our resurrection experiences come close to our eternal living in God, but they concretize the hope we have for a future where we will live from glory to glory (see 2 Cor 3:18). Resurrection is experienced not only when we see a bad situation through to a good and graced end, but also when we refuse to participate in moral evil from the start. When, through grace, we triumph over temptation, resurrection is known in the conquering of the ego. The resurrected life teaches us that there is life after sin. We can go on and live fully after conversion despite our fears that conversion will cost us too much. Christ's death for sin and His resurrection give us the hope to die to our sin and come out on the other side, in triumph through our trust in Him. Moral conversion can occur because we know we can rise after sin in the power of Christ's resurrection.

Eucharist and Gratitude

The Catholic should above all be a person of gratitude. This virtue deepens within us as we regularly recall the mercy of God as offered to us in Christ. Each Sunday we are given the opportunity to recall this merciful love of God as we participate in worship. Beyond this, we can make an examination of conscience each day that not only includes acknowledgement of sins that plague us (see 2 Cor 12:7), but also recognizes the graces of the day. We can learn to recall these graces so that cynicism and sarcasm do not replace the hope and gratitude that are our birthright as baptized people. To live a grateful life, we must cultivate an acute awareness of the present moment of grace. We need to take up the discipline of recalling these graces, which refresh us in times of difficulty or pain. God often draws very near to us, but we cannot grow in intimacy with Him if we are not aware of the present moment of grace, or if we quickly lose sight of it due to the daily struggles and cares of family and professional life.

I recall one grace that marked a new beginning for me of remembering the ordinary visitations of God. When my son Kristoffer was a little boy of three, he came to me to ask if we could go outside and play. He was interrupting some studying I was doing at the kitchen table, so I am sure I looked perturbed. "Maybe later," I said hoping to brush him away. He left and came back about five minutes later, "Now?" "Okay," I said, getting up from the table, "but we are just going around the block for a short walk, do you understand?" But Kristoffer didn't hear me — he was already at the door, eager to get underway. We went out into the cool spring air. My mind was still on my work back at the table, so it took me a little while to realize how slowly we were moving. "Come on, Kris, we have to get going; Dad has a lot of work to do." Kristoffer was not interested in my projects or self-imposed deadlines; he was interested in being alive. Every couple of steps he would stop and stoop over to touch something, smell something, look more closely at something. I was harassing him, "Move," as well as tolerating him, "That's nice, Kris." But he was *contemplating*. I suddenly stopped and realized that he was really taken up into this walk. He was not living in the past or the future as I was; he was living in the present. I began to think that this kind of living is what prayer is all about. I realized that I hadn't been quite so tuned in to the present moment in a very long time. Even when I was studying, I was doing so in order to teach a good class, or write a good article to be published, or please one of my graduate professors. I didn't study to learn; I studied to get something else. Kristoffer was simply studying rocks and bugs and blades of grass because they caught his attention. He was in no hurry to rush beyond the present, because that's where he lived and was happy. I began to wonder if I had ever lived in the present. "Live in the present and know God and yourself, Dad" — that's what my three-year-old spiritual director was teaching me. After this lesson I began to pray that I would slow down and watch with Kris, to touch plants with Kris, and be grateful with Kris.

I wrote this lesson down in a small journal so that I could recall that one must try to live in the present if one wishes to be happy. Kris was saying, "What's the rush, Dad? Live here with me on this walk; those books of yours will be there when we return home." Similarly, I recall a famous Fordham philosopher, Norris Clarke, closing a presentation once by imploring his listeners to stop *taking* from life and instead *receive* life gratefully. He bid us farewell by suggesting, "Let a walk take you somewhere, let a drink of water take you somewhere, let a bath take you. . . . We Americans are always taking, let's allow ourselves to be taken instead."

Not too long after the birth of our second son, Jonathan, I went to the local park with my boys. Jonathan was in a Snugli to keep him warm, a sack-like support that positioned him comfortably on my chest. When we arrived at the park, Kristoffer ran toward the slide screaming with delight. Up and down the slide he went, never stopping to see what else the park offered. He shouted with joy each time he went down the slide. I watched him closely from a nearby swing. I sat on the swing gliding gently and holding Jonathan close. I moved my hand from Jonathan's back to his head. When I touched his small round head and pressed him gently against my chest, I began to cry. In seeing Kristoffer's joy and feeling Jonathan so close to me, I was suddenly gifted with my new identity as a father. At that moment I became aware of the awesome truth that I was a father and that these boys were mine to raise, cherish, and then send off on their own journeys into holiness. As I sat there on the swing, I was quietly led into prayer, gratefully praising God for this small share in His own Fatherhood. By receiving the truth of that moment in the park and not trying to take or control the time there, I was led into my own fatherhood. The truth of who I was *took me*, and I am grateful.

Love of Neighbor

As I mentioned earlier in this book, the meaning of life is found in loving God, self, and others. Our neighbors cry out with their needs and we are called to serve them. In serving we are liberated from a life of dry self-centeredness, which, if left unrestrained, provokes boredom and restlessness. The way to freedom is to *be for others*. The American culture, however, teaches that the way to freedom is to exercise one's ability to choose between many alternatives, to morally "shop around." This vision of freedom is heavily influenced by our market mentality. We feel we need choices and variety, even if those choices are as superficial as product selections or the number of channels on our television sets. Real moral freedom resides not in choice among alternatives but in knowing what is good and loving it. This means, for example, that we choose only one spouse and love him or her until death. And it means we stay faithful in service to the needs of fellow parishioners. Jesus did not ask us to live manic, superficial, mobile lives — just faithful lives of simple service. The call from Christ as we grow in our baptismal identity is to go deep, not broad (see Lk 5:4). There really are people who "live in the middle of nowhere" rather than New York, Paris, or Rome, and who, upon their deathbeds, recount a rich and noble life because they understood that in having loved they touched the divine.

The paradoxical thing about Americans' love of choice and frenetic activity is that we have created a choice-less society. In the city where I live, developers are replicating every grocery store, restaurant, mall, and department store in all of its quadrants. With each new mall there is actually nothing new to look forward to, since we know that the businesses therein will simply be more of the same. We have many malls, stores, and restaurants to choose from, *but they are all the same.* The east side of the city looks like the north and the west and the south. I know we find comfort in familiar surroundings, but, from to a variety of economic reasons, there is no real variety, choice, or imagination left in the business of creating consumers. We have become what we most dread in this entertainment-soaked culture — boring. We have no choices, except to *conform* to the dictates of those who develop our land and cities. Perhaps one of the reasons we resent conforming to what is morally good is that choosing right and wrong is actually the *only* choice we have left. "At least here," we unconsciously think, "I will exercise my ability to say 'no.' " Our culture tells us we all *have* to live in urban sprawl, we all *have* to wear certain clothes, we all *have* to have certain hobbies or play certain sports, and we all *have* to go to college and get married. Enough! There is only one thing *necessary*, and "Mary has chosen the better part" (Lk 10:42). Our task, our *only* task as Christians, is to contemplate Jesus and obey his greatest commandment — "love one another" (Jn 15:17).

To choose to love neighbor is to exercise the most formative of moral activities. In this activity we are molded to become the witnesses that Jesus intended when He called us at baptism (see Jn 13:35). The mark of the Christian is a love that chooses the good of others out of the power of being first loved by God. Loving others is a testament to the One who has first loved us, and loving in this way is only sustained by prayer and contemplation. This is a pious statement, and it is likely to remain only a platitude if we do not actually desire to enter into the kind of life made possible by grace. One tragedy of parish life is that we tend to think those who love others are phonies or showoffs rather than witnesses to be emulated. Simply because we do not always exhibit virtuous behavior, perhaps out of self-hate, we sometimes judge those who *do* to be frauds or hypocrites. We shouldn't measure others' abilities to love by our own possibly diminished capabilities. There is a love out there that is beyond our imagining, and some in our communities tap into it and make decisions out of it and eventually become one with what the "eye has not seen, and ear has not heard" (1 Cor 2:9).

This is how Jesus saves us from sin. He so transforms our minds and sense of freedom[28] that we begin to truly worship Him and are then directed toward the needs of others. When we adore God, He blesses us with intimacy but then calls us to serve the needs of those in our parishes. This is the beauty of God: We contemplate God, but God doesn't smother us in His being or hold us only to Himself. God directs us to Himself and *then to other persons*. Others are always included in our love for God.

I remember the first novel that really moved me, Stephen Crane's *The Red Badge of Courage*, which I read in junior high school. I recall the compassion it evoked in me for the soldiers and victims of war. It also pricked my conscience with questions about war's futility and horror. After I finished reading it, however, I went back to it only once. Its words of beauty didn't become the *only* words I sought. In fact, in being awakened to beauty by its words, I sought out other books voraciously. This is what true beauty does for us. It would be strange to come upon a man admiring a painting at an art museum and return years later to find him still riveted to that same painting. The natural course of having communion with what is beautiful is to become more expansive, more open, and more hospitable to other things, persons, and experiences of beauty. God's beauty is like that, and the effect of knowing God is to be invited by him to know the beauty of other persons as well.

The standard, however, for what is beautiful from God's viewpoint is different from what our popular culture or intellectual sophistication now dictates. St. Francis of Assisi learned quite painfully what the beauty of God looks like in his creatures. The biographers of Francis tell the story of his aversion to lepers — Francis was reported to "feel sick" in their presence. St. Bonaventure writes that Francis remembered "his need to overcome himself first" and eventually ran up and kissed a leper's hand after placing a coin in it.[29] The new standard that God gives for beauty is found in this act of remembering to overcome the self first, so as then to be able to love one's neighbor. We overcome the self, really our selfishness, by actually serving others. And, Francis didn't turn away from the leper and go home to think about overcoming his selfishness, in order to come back another day to serve the leper. He wanted to overcome selfishness while it still possessed him. The only way he saw fit to grow out of his selfishness was to actually serve someone in need. The move to act in the face of another's need is vital to service and to growth in moral virtue. Its execution is a thing of beauty.

I remember a time when my wife, my sons, and I were visiting New York City. I was raised there, and one decision I made years ago was never to give cash handouts to street beggars. I had rationalized this with all the stock reasons: "They will only spend it on alcohol; they should get a job; it doesn't really solve their problems; they make more money begging than some employed people do; and so on." It was not until this trip, however, that I passed a New York City beggar while in the company of my two small sons. Kristoffer and Jonathan saw only need and poverty. They heard only the words, "Can you spare some change?" At one point we passed by Grand Central Station, where some beggars were seated on the sidewalk. Several feet past them, Kristoffer grabbed my coat and asked, "Dad, didn't you give him any money?" As I looked into my son's face, all the reasons I had used for not giving to the poor on the street suddenly meant nothing. "You're right," I said, "I'll go back and give him something." Kristoffer and Jonathan walked back with me (to make sure I was really going to go through with it?!). I put some coins into the man's sack that lay on the sidewalk. He looked up from the ground and said, "God bless you." "You see," said Jonathan, "God will bless you now." Since then, I have never passed by another beggar without giving him or her some money. Through the eyes of children, I saw that my theories on whether almsgiving was a truly productive way to assist the homeless didn't matter. And all of sudden I didn't really care whether it was effective or not. Someone was in need and asked for help. My boys taught me to respond to my neighbor's need and not ignore them under the pretense of thinking I knew what was best for them. My boys taught me that I had made a wrong choice in passing by the poor. In fact, I am beginning to believe that, like Mary contemplating Jesus, responding to people's *needs* is the one thing necessary in the moral realm (see Lk 10:41).

Of course, giving money to the poor on the street doesn't cost much — only a glance and the movement necessary for locating pocket change. Love of neighbor is known in the habitual care and concern shown to others on a regular basis, in order that concern for the good of others becomes part of one's character. That is what following Christ is about — choosing to love regularly and thus being created into someone who *does* love and therefore is like Christ. In becoming loving persons through our loving actions, we become Christ to others.

These four mysteries of crucifixion, resurrection, gratitude, and love of neighbor, known in the context of a life of Catholic worship, make up the ingredients for a Catholic moral mind. The more we live out of these events and truths, the more we will make trustworthy decisions about right and wrong. When we fall short, we are always to call upon the mercy of God. The conversion of our consciences to love what is good can be a slow, consistent process of growth, or it can be jump-started into life by a sudden insight into one's own or the community's need for repentance. Either way, the conscience needs to be nourished by the Eucharist, which is the embodiment of all four of these Christian mysteries as they are present in the host of the Mass, Jesus Christ Himself.

8

Struggling to Be Good

Ultimately, what the Catholic needs to do in his or her moral life, by way of moral formation in the parish, is to seek purity of heart. This purity is not to be construed narrowly as pertaining only to lustful desires. It includes this of course, but fundamentally to have a pure heart is to be one who views all moral living through the interior conversation we have with Christ in our conscience. Purity of heart is, in the end, a life of prayer manifested as moral living. Listening to our conscience, which is inclined to listen to Christ, becomes the prayer of our hearts. The heart needs to be purified because we are free in our choices and in our loves. We may, in fact, have chosen poorly, and on some occasions we may have chosen to love what is beneath our dignity. This kind of loving may include a disordered affection for pleasing the ego, satisfying our lustful desires, or quenching our thirst for power and control. The heart may also have grown to hate what we really should love: God, our neighbor, and ourselves. These attitudes and habits need to be purified, and our hearts need to attend to the heart of the Savior and nothing less.

The German theologian Karl Rahner once wrote, "That the inmost core of personal reality is love and that love is in fact the inmost reality, this is experienced by man only in coming to know the heart of the Lord."[30] Since the love of God has taken up eternal residence in the heart of Christ, contemplating Christ's heart contains a powerful, symbolic energy that focuses the believer upon the very core of reality and thus purifies any idolatrous or sinful habits. The heart needs to be pure in order to hear the word of God regarding what is right or wrong for this particular person in this particular situation. As Christians, we should not be blindly obedient to authority, nor should we be striving for some rationalistic objectivity devoid of faith or spirituality. It is in turning the heart toward a prayerful dialogue with Christ that enables the conscience to best apprehend the morally true decision.

Ultimately, moral decisions are the responsibility of the person or community that makes them. If we decide incorrectly, only our own limitations and sin can be to blame. Of course, there may be justifiable excuses mitigating blame. Purity of heart, however, is the work of the ordinary moral life of the Catholic — it is something for which we should all strive. This purity is achieved through trial and error, a commitment to prayer, and practicing the virtues. There is no magic formula, rather only the commitment that comes from being authentically in love with God and deriving one's inspiration for moral choosing from that love.

Only those who are pure of heart will see God (see Mt 5:8 and Ps 24:4).[31] Only those who seek God's face and seek to live a life which bears the stamp of one who has seen the divine face can stand in the holy place (see 1 Sam 6:20), the place of worship. Christians don't have to be morally perfect to approach God, but we do have to *desire* to become good and turn from sin. This is simply a matter of honesty. We do not want to say that we follow the Lord but then continue in ways of living that contradict the clear teachings and virtues he expressed in the Scriptures. The goal of moral formation in the Catholic parish is to assist parishioners to "love from a pure heart, a good conscience, and a sincere faith" (1 Tim 1:5).

Paul Wadell has written that the Eucharist invites us into a life of moral purity, a life with a cleansed heart and clear vision. We learn through worship to see clearly and love what is worthy of our affections. The remembering we do in the liturgy of Christ's paschal mystery is a participation not only in his life, death, and resurrection, but also in our own moral reform.[32]

> The strategy of the Eucharist, like the strategy of Christian morality, is to let God come fully to life in us. . . . This is why Christian morality and the liturgy ultimately are one, and why the Eucharist is the most morally charged event in the Christian life. Through the Eucharist we not only change, we become Godly — we take on the mind of Christ — and Christian morality wants nothing less.[33]

This sentiment of Wadell's is quite compelling. "*The Eucharist is the most morally charged event in the Christian life*"! To see this point is to see clearly the core of Christian reality. Parishioners are encouraged toward holiness and moral goodness in order to unleash the power of God's life within them. To be good is to be one with God. That is all we are about as human beings. To be one with God is our deepest desire. The question which faith poses to us is whether we believe this. Do we believe that the meaning of human existence is found in communion with God in Christ, and that the virtue and behavior that flows from this communion is the essence of Christian ethics? We have to discern the choices before us with the mind of Christ. When we partake in the Body and Blood of Christ, we are altered; we are changed into His Body and Blood for the world. We testify to Him, witness for Him through our character. It is this character that is formed by the ritual prayer of being vulnerable to God's Word and sacrament and letting God affect us by His holiness.

Struggling to Live the Moral Truth

It is no secret that some can also testify that, after living according to the moral doctrine of the Church for years, they gave it up. To those who left the moral life as understood by Catholicism, what can we say? Is it a matter of saying to them that they should have tried harder, trusted more? On the surface these exhortations can seem naïve. Those who did try and were crushed under some weight can give testimonials, persuading others to agree that the moral life is too burdensome. Identifying that weight is difficult indeed. Was it the person's own weakness (not enough faith?)? Or was the doctrine objectively wrong? This is why many in the Catholic Church are calling for a change or a development in moral doctrine, especially in the area of sexual and medical ethics. Very few Catholics, many rightly claim, are convinced by the moral teachings of the Church in these areas. It is said that since "no one" is living these teachings, especially regarding sexual ethics, it seems reasonable to change them and let people live in good conscience. We are, then, at an impasse.

The bishops appear unconvinced that change in some moral doctrine is possible. Those who disagree and want to update say, "Wake up and look around; no one is listening. Maybe the moral doctrines we teach do not carry the force of truth, and therefore cannot persuade." How can we come together again, as a community of conscience, if so many in the community are not having their consciences formed by faith's doctrine?

Can we renew the Church morally? Can those who disagree with Church teaching abide with those who embrace it, and still find friendship with one another in Christ?

The question of alienation from the moral truths of Catholicism is complex because it is the result of so many competing factors and allegiances. Certainly those who are in disagreement with the Church's moral teachings are still welcome in Catholic parishes. How will moral conversion or the development of doctrine ever take place if people cannot immerse themselves in communal prayer and the Word proclaimed? Those who disagree with doctrine and practice behavior that the Church identifies as "objectively immoral" may find my comment urging hospitality quaint at best or hypocritical at worst. "We don't need your welcome," they might say; "We are convinced of God's love and of our certitude regarding the issues we dissent over." The more difficult question asked by pastoral leaders is this: When does a dissenter become a prophet? Or alternately, can one dissent on so many moral issues as to no longer be a Catholic, practically speaking?

If a dissenter is to become a prophet, the very teachers — the bishops — who now hold the aspiring moral prophet in abeyance must recognize his or her prophetic vocation. It is common practice for revisionist moral thinkers to point out how the bishops rejected some of the ideas of theologians who later became the advisors to bishops at the Second Vatican Council. They usually raise this point to illustrate the fact that the magisterium can make mistakes in its judgments of theological and pastoral ideas.[34] The irony is that the very ones who rejected theologians like Karl Rahner, Yves Congar, John Courtney Murray, and Henri de Lubac are the ones who invited them into service at the Council, namely the bishops. If revisionist theologians are ever to be revered by the Church as moral prophets possessing great foresight, it will, paradoxically, have to be the very body of people who now reject their controversial positions — the bishops — who come to define them as doctrine. The people can recognize prophets, but the hierarchy must *establish* them. Those who dissent from Church moral teaching recognize this or they wouldn't so admire the pre-Vatican II theologians whose ideas about doctrine were finally recognized as truthful (such as the acceptability of interfaith prayer and interdenominational marriages).

Furthermore, to date the most controversial positions urging acceptance of birth control, artificial reproduction, divorce and remarriage, and gay marriages have not been approved by the magisterium. Equally, although the majority of citizens are in favor of the death penalty, Pope John Paul II and the bishops of the world see little moral justification to ever enact a capital death sentence.[35] To argue for the development of doctrine on the first set of moral questions is to be aligned with the political left. Alternately, to stand in favor of capital punishment is to be aligned with the political right. Neither of these political labels is sufficient for defending a *Catholic position* on these issues. Catholics are faith-filled first and only accidentally politically left or right.

To be of a Catholic mind is to be one who has listened to the bishops with deep respect; and it is to be one who has further recognized that one's own personal judgment regarding a particular issue may not be reflective of the whole truth for a community. In other words, it is possible that some people may be arguing for a development in church moral teaching because they want the community, through its leadership, to affirm their own moral weakness. Others may simply be unable to give assent to a doctrine because they do not see the truth of the Church's position; but, this inability to see the truth may in fact be blindness due to years of acting against church teaching. Persons may resist embracing moral doctrine because to *not* resist may put their whole life in question in the face of the content of the Church's teachings. This reality could be too difficult for some to deal with and so, rather than seek conversion and the upheaval this would cause in their lives, they continue to be in favor of activities that contradict moral truth.

Beyond this, some moral doctrines contain different or more inclusive realities in their assessment of right and wrong than popular culture will allow. This is certainly true in the area of sexual ethics. In this area, our culture exalts privacy and choice as the key moral norms. The Church's vision of sex is broader and deeper than this, including concern for fidelity, fecundity, sacramental symbolism, and embodiment. I remember giving a workshop to teenagers on moral decision-making using a case study on gay marriages in order to illustrate for them the Catholic meaning of sexual ethics. In our discussion, I stated the Church's position against homosexual activity. The room of teens responded as one: "What right does the Church have to tell others what to do with their bodies in private?" As Americans we can recognize two major cultural values within that statement: individual rights (choice) and privacy. For many Americans, the two values of rights and privacy supersede any value the Church may see in the reproductive meaning and complementary nature of sex. According to the teens, the Church should stay out of moral decision-making, as long as no one involved in the behavior gets hurt. Of course, by saying this, the persons mean physically or emotionally hurt. But pastoral ministers need to raise awareness within persons of the reality of *spiritual* and *moral* harm, as well as the physical and emotional harm to which persons are already well-attuned. The sensibility that sin is a harm is hardly alive within some persons. Sin simply appears to them as a subjective judgment of ecclesial leadership. They say, "We will instead trust in the current culture and in the love that God has for everyone." "Of course God loves everyone," the weary minister may respond, "but every act that these beloved engage in cannot be assumed into the goodness and truth of Who God is."

Finally, people may disagree with the moral teachings of the Church simply because they are convinced the truth is not in them.

In this case, personal character is not blocking one's ability to see these truths. Instead, the teaching is just not true and one's conscience will not allow one to embrace it. This position is the one that more often than not draws this response from pastoral leaders: "Oh, you disagree; I had better leave you to your conscience." It seems to me that leaving a fellow Catholic to his or her conscience is the *last step* of pastoral ministry, not the first. And even if there is nothing more to be done in the public forum (teaching, counseling, retreat, study, etc.) in order to test the authenticity of the disagreement, respecting an individual's conscientious dissent does not mean isolating the person from parish life. The responsibility of the parish always is to call out to those on the margins of Catholic moral living. The primary question becomes one of conversion: Am I open to being convinced by the Spirit that my behavior, attitude, or disposition is wrong? No one is beyond the call of humility. And this call is to be vibrantly alive in the Catholic life. For those who are convinced in conscience that the moral teaching of the Church is wrong: You have a responsibility, as far as virtue allows, to remain with the parish in prayer, study, and acts of charity. For those whose consciences are convinced of the truth of ecclesial moral doctrine: You have a responsibility to humbly abide with and invite those who disagree into deeper prayer, study, and fellowship.

The goal is to set our hearts upon the Lord, who will purify us in the light of his merciful love and bracing truth. It is a struggle to trust God enough to be vulnerable before this mercy and truth. In this struggle we fear losing the self and the world as we know it. But Christ has taught us to trust him in our moral journey because he has "overcome the world"— those sinful aspects of living that remain obstacles to communion with God (see Jn 16:33).

Conclusion

To see that the Eucharist is the most morally charged event in the Christian life is to identify the place where moral conversion can occur and/or where moral virtue can be deepened. Whether we appropriate the moral doctrine of the Church as our own or whether we withhold assent to its content, all Catholics are called to be active participants in the formative worship of the Mass. In this worship, our deepest virtues are formed and our deepest questions are answered over time.

The moral life is not the *only* aspect of our faith. But all other aspects of this faith — Scripture, worship, service, and vocation — should inform the moral life. The central pastoral task is to continue to proclaim Christ in and out of season, because Christian moral conversion is only possible through the (re)evangelization of conscience. In this evangelization lies the answer to deepening our virtues and casting out erroneous thoughts and behavior. The evangelized moral life is one based upon a positive encounter between Christ and the conscience, and not a heavy-handed run-in with ecclesiastical law. Moral dissent will always be with us. Achieving moral authenticity, however, can only be accomplished in the fullness of a life drawn from the ecclesial Christ, not simply the opinions of political parties and trends.

I began this book by noting that our deepest desire is to be good because no one wants to fail as a human being. If we place our lives trustingly within the mysteries of Christ, any chance for failure in the human adventure becomes slim indeed. Moral renewal has its source in a person falling in love with the Good. This ancient philosophical idea was personalized with the coming of Christ, Who put a face on the Good. If we love what is good, we are loving Christ. As Christians we can go to Christ explicitly and ask Him to help us love what He loves and see what He sees.

Endnotes

1. See M. Scott Peck, *People of the Lie: The Hope for Healing Human Evil* (New York: Simon and Schuster, 1983). Throughout this section I rely on some of Peck's insights into the nature of moral evil, particularly as found in chapters 2, 3, and 4.

2. Paul Wadell, *The Primacy of Love* (Mahwah, NJ: Paulist Press, 1992), 35.

3. Robert Coles, *The Moral Intelligence of Children* (New York: Random House, 1997), 20-25.

4. Gilbert Meilander, *The Theory and Practice of Virtue* (Notre Dame, IN: University of Notre Dame Press, 1984), 83.

5. See Dick Westly, *Morality and its Beyond* (Mystic, CT: Twenty-Third Publications, 1985), 18-27.

6. See Richard B. Hays, *The Moral Vision of the New Testament* (San Francisco: Harper, 1996), 45.

7. Coles, 31.

8. *Gaudium et Spes* (Pastoral Constitution on the Church in the Modern World), 16. See Catholic Church, Second Vatican Council, *Vatican Council II: The Conciliar and Post Conciliar Documents*, ed. Austin Flannery (Wilmington: Scholarly Resources, 1975).

9. Meilander, 83.

10. See Lawrence Cunningham's books on Catholicism, particularly: *Catholic Experience: Space, Time, Silence, Prayer, Sacraments, Story, Persons, Catholicity, Community, and Expectations* (New York: Crossroad, 1985) and *Catholic Heritage: Martyrs, Ascetics, Pilgrims, Warriors, Mystics, Theologians, Artists, Humanists, Activists, Outsiders, and Saints* (New York: Crossroad, 1983).

11. See Todd Salzman, "Catholicism and Colonialism: The Church's Failure in Rwanda," *Commonweal* 124:10 (May 23, 1997), 17-19.

12. Catholic Church, *Catechism of the Catholic Church* (Vatican City: Libreria Editrice Vaticana, 1994), 1337.

13. Mark O'Keefe, O.S.B., *Becoming Good, Becoming Holy: On the Relationship of Christian Ethics and Spirituality* (New York: Paulist Press, 1995), 141.

14. John Paul II, *Veritatis Splendor* (The Splendor of Truth) (Vatican City: Libreria Editrice Vaticana, 1993), 64.

15. Jean Porter, "The Subversion of Virtue," *Annual of the Society of Christian Ethics*, ed. Harlan Beckley (Boston: Society of Christian Ethics, 1992), 37.

16. Augustine, St. *Faith, Hope and Charity*, tr. Louis A. Arand (Westminster, MD: Newman Press, 1963), 81.

17. See James Hanigan, "Conversion and Christian Ethics," in R.P. Hamel and K.R. Himes, eds., *Introduction to Christian Ethics: A Reader* (New York: Paulist Press, 1989), 242-250.

18. Associated Press, "Ex-presidential adviser Morris says arrogance led to downfall," *Columbus (Ohio) Dispatch*, 24 Nov. 1996, A13.

19. AP, *Columbus Dispatch*, A13.

20. Peck, 77-83.

21. Peck, 177.

22. Robert Bellah, et al., *Habits of the Heart: Individualism and Commitment in American Life* (Berkeley: University of California Press, 1985), 71-75.

23. See Arlie Russell Hochschild, "There's No Place Like Work," *The New York Times Magazine* (April 20, 1997), 50-55, 81, 84. See also John F. Kavanaugh, *Following Christ In A Consumer Society Still: The Spirituality of Cultural Resistance* (Maryknoll, NY: Orbis Books, 1991).

24. John Paul II, *Dives in misericordia* (Rich in Mercy) (Hales Corners, WI: Priests of the Sacred Heart, 1981), 4. Encyclical, November 30, 1980.

25. John Paul II, *Evangelium Vitae* (The Gospel of Life) (Vatican City: Libreria Editrice Vaticana, 1995), 19.

26. *Veritatis Splendor,* 40.

27. Walter Kasper, *Theology and Church* (New York: Crossroad, 1989), 90.

28. See Luke Timothy Johnson, "How Does Jesus Save Us?" *Priests and People* 11 (April 1997), 129-133.

29. Bonaventure, St., "Major Life of St. Francis," in Marion Habig, ed., *St. Francis of Assisi: Writings and Early Biographies; English omnibus of the Sources for the Life of St. Francis* (Chicago: Franciscan Herald Press, 1973) ch. 1, n. 5, pp. 638-639.

30. Karl Rahner, " 'Behold this Heart!': Preliminaries to a Theology of Devotion to the Sacred Heart," *Theological Investigations*, vol. 3 (New York: Crossroad, 1982), 327.

31. Prov 22:11; 1 Tim 1:5, 5:22; 1 Pet 3:2; 2 Tim 2:22; Ps 24:4.

32. Paul Wadell, C.P., "What Do All Those Masses Do For Us?" in Kathleen Hughes and Mark Francis, eds., *Living No Longer For Ourselves: Liturgy and Justice in the Nineties* (Collegeville, MN: Liturgical Press, 1991), 161.

33. Wadell, "What Do All Those Masses Do For Us?", 162.

34. Thomas J. Reese, S.J., writes: "Many bishops blame this division in the church on dissenters and the press. In fact, the hierarchy itself must take much of the blame for the low state of its credibility. During the last three decades, time and time again prominent cardinals have attacked proposed reforms as disastrous for the church. Religious liberty, ecumenism, collegiality, meat on Friday, vernacular liturgies, giving the cup to the laity, Communion in the hand and altar girls were fought and delayed by members of the hierarchy who condemned the proponents of these changes as people who wanted to destroy the church. Throughout history, the hierarchy has often been its own worst enemy. It has condemned or silenced theologians (like Jesuit Fr. John Courtney Murray) who were later honored by the church. These rash condemnations not only alienated liberals but also conservatives, who felt betrayed when the bishops finally changed their minds. With this record of first condemning and then switching, it is no surprise that people do not take the church's current condemnations seriously." Thomas F. Reese, S.J., "2001 and Beyond: Preparing the Church for the Next Millennium," *America* 176 (June 21-28, 1997), 14.

35. See *Evangelium Vitae*, 56.